Journey Through Wales

by Roger Thomas

GALLERY BOOKS
An Imprint of W. H. Smith Publishers Inc.
112 Madison Avenue
New York City 10016

Endpapers: The still waters of Llyn Cregennen,
near Dolgellau
Title page: The conical towers of Castle Coch
in South Glamorgan
Title verso/Introduction: The Elan Valley
lakelands, Powys
Contents page: Harlech Castle seen amid the
rugged countryside of Gwynedd

Editor: Donna Wood
Art Editor: Edward Pitcher
Designer: Steve Wilson
Maps: Eugene Fleury
Production: Steve Roberts

Produced by Marshall Cavendish Books Limited.
Published by
GALLERY BOOKS
An imprint of W.H. Smith Publishers Inc.
112 Madison Avenue, New York,
New York 10016
©Marshall Cavendish Limited 1986

ISBN 0-8317-5263-7

Typeset in Palatino by TypeFast Ltd, London
Printed in Italy by L.E.G.O. S.p.a. Vicenza

Introduction

Wales, less than 200 miles from north to south, is a small country of unparalleled scenic variety, reflected in its three very different national parks. Snowdonia's 835 square miles embrace the highest mountains in England and Wales; 225-square-mile Pembrokeshire is the only coastal national park in Britain; and the Brecon Beacons' 520 square miles are filled with green, open flanks and swooping mountain crests.

Then there are Wales's four 'Areas of Outstanding Natural Beauty': the Wye Valley together with the coastlines around the Isle of Anglesey and along the Gower and Lleyn Peninsulas.

Collectively, the people of Wales insist on proclaiming, and maintaining, their Welsh identity. Individually, their notions of Welshness rarely coincide. The culture here is a complex one, as even the most cursory look at Wales's convoluted history will reveal. Traditional Wales, bound up in the survival of the ancient Welsh language, casts a wary eye over its shoulder at events elsewhere. City kids from cosmopolitan Cardiff are now more familiar with computers than coracles.

Wales, a coat of many colours, throws up paradoxes and contradictions aplenty – and manages to accommodate them all. Quite how this conjuring trick is performed is a complete mystery. The cantankerous Welsh were, remember, once renowned for their wizardry.

Contents

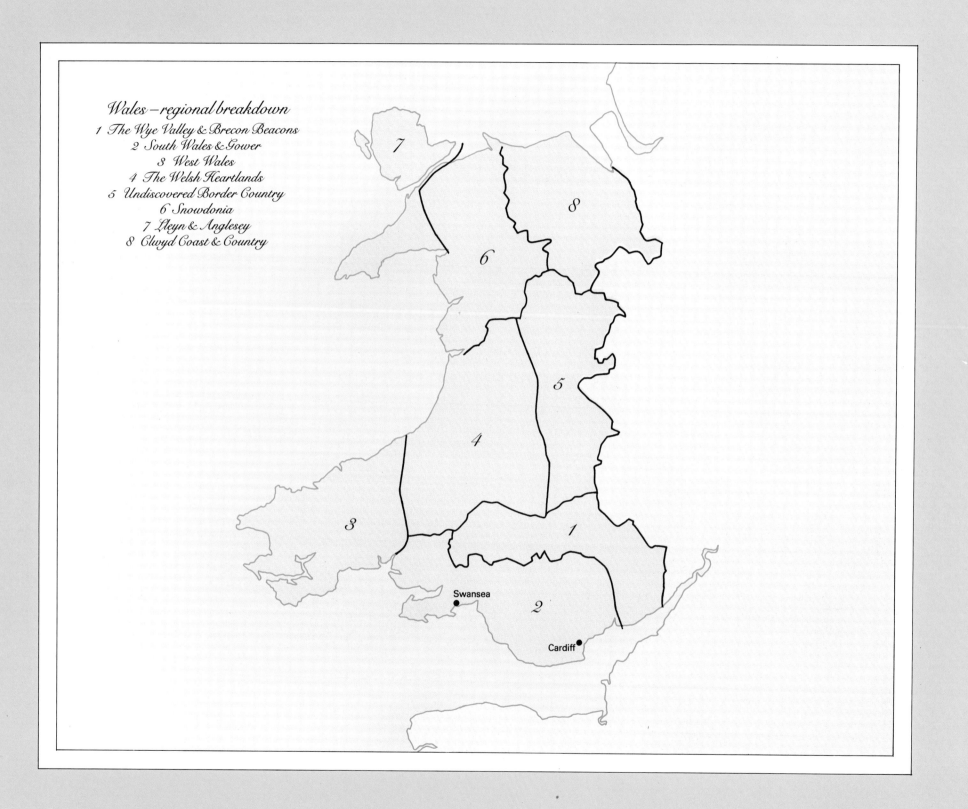

Wales – regional breakdown
1 *The Wye Valley & Brecon Beacons*
2 *South Wales & Gower*
3 *West Wales*
4 *The Welsh Heartlands*
5 *Undiscovered Border Country*
6 *Snowdonia*
7 *Lleyn & Anglesey*
8 *Clwyd Coast & Country*

Swansea

Cardiff

The Wye Valley & Brecon Beacons

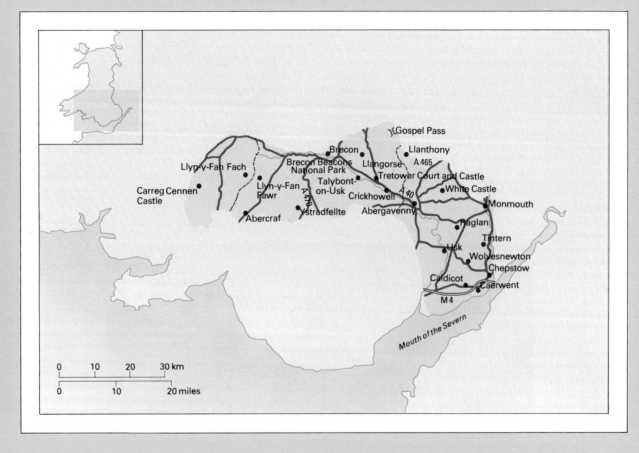

Left: Dramatic skies over one of Wales's most dramatic castles. Carreg Cennen, perched on a lonely outcrop in the brooding Black Mountain

Map labels: Gospel Pass · Brecon · Llanthony · A 465 · Llyn-y-Fan Fach · Brecon Beacons National Park · Llangorse · Tretower Court and Castle · Carreg Cennen Castle · Llyn-y-Fan Fawr · Talybont-on-Usk · White Castle · Crickhowell · A 40 · Monmouth · Abercraf · Ystradfellte · Abergavenny · Raglan · Tintern · Usk · Wolvesnewton · Chepstow · Caldicot · Caerwent · M 4 · Mouth of the Severn

Scale: 0 10 20 30 km · 0 10 20 miles

AS REPRESENTED ON the map, the Wye Valley north of the medieval gateway town of Chepstow does nothing more than define the line of the border between Wales and England. Closer acquaintance reveals a lovely, leafy vale, its riverbanks and wooded hillsides protected as an 'Area of Outstanding Natural Beauty'.

Few will quarrel with this official description. There is no better introduction to Wales than the drive north from Chepstow. Open meadowland soon narrows into the sinuous, shady confines of the Wye Valley. The valley opens out again at Monmouth into undulating, undisturbed border country, a patchwork of farmlands dotted with pretty towns and villages. The ebb and flow of Welsh history has washed across these strategic borderlands, leaving Roman remains and castles.

The busy market town of Abergavenny is another gateway, standing at the entrance to the Brecon Beacons National Park. The park — all 520 square miles of it — sweeps across much of southern Wales from the Black Mountains, which straddle the border, to the similarly named, but entirely separate Black Mountain in the far west.

The Beacons themselves occupy centre stage, their fresh and windy flanks rising to nearly 3000 ft at Pen-y-fan, South Wales's highest peak. Unlike the rocky mountains in the north of Wales, the Brecon Beacons ars smooth and green. A string of lakes and pockets of pine forest are dwarfed by big skies, huge views and unbroken horizons.

ABERCRAF
Powys

Two attractive places to visit are located next door to each other within the confines of the narrow, steep-sided Upper Tawe Valley near this village. The 40-acre Craig-y-Nos Country Park, by the banks of the river, is a pleasant, ornamental parkland of specimen trees, open meadowland, lake and pond.

It was designed as a 'pleasure ground' for the 19th-century opera singer, Madame Adelina Patti. The park was an accompaniment to her home, a rambling sham castle of monumental proportions which is now a home for the elderly.

The limestone outcrops in the hillside above the castle mark the entrance of the Dan-yr-Ogof caves. This showcave complex, which claims to be the largest in western Europe, contains no less than three separate systems open to the public. Guided tours in the main showcave just scratch the surface of a vast and labrynthine network of caves, discovered in 1912, which extends for miles into the mountain. A second entrance leads to the Cathedral Cavern, 160 ft long by 70 ft high. Further up the hillside is the architecturally fascinating 'Bone Cave', which tells the story of its occupation by man and beast from prehistoric times.

 *BOTH ATTRACTIONS are located on the A4067, 20 miles northeast of Swansea.*

ABERGAVENNY
Gwent

This busy town, surrounded by farms and fields in the pastoral Vale of Usk, retains its long established links with the countryside. The farming community still comes to town every Tuesday for important livestock sales, held in the market place behind the bustling main street.

Abergavenny Castle, a scant ruin dating from the 12th century, overlooks green fields and meadows leading down to the Usk. Today, it seems unthinkable that this pleasant spot was the scene of a treacherous murder on the Christmas of 1176 when the infamous Norman lord William de Braose invited an unsuspecting group of Welsh noblemen to a banquet, killing them whilst unarmed.

Abergavenny's backdrop of rolling hills and mountains is a beautiful one, dominated by the distinctive shape of the 1955 ft Sugar Loaf.

ABERGAVENNY can be reached on the A4042 from Newport, the A40 from Raglan and the A465 'Heads of the Valleys' road from Merthyr.

BRECON
Powys

The narrow streets of this ancient market town are now thankfully by-passed by through traffic. Brecon's charter was granted in 1270, at which time it was ruled by its hilltop castle, now an intriguing ruin, partly incorporated into the Castle Hotel.

Brecon's Welsh name, *Aberhonddu* ('Mouth of the River Honddu'), reflects its location at the confluence of the Honddu and Usk. Twice-weekly markets, on Tuesdays and Fridays, perpetuate its strong links with the farming community and genuine, country town atmosphere. Brecon is also a natural centre for the Brecon Beacons National Park. The park's three main upland areas — the wild Black Mountain in the west, the central Beacons, and the borderland Black Mountains — are all within easy reach. The main headquarters for the park are in the town. And Pen-y-fan, its highest peak, dominates the horizon to the south.

Brecknock Museum displays a marvellous collection of Welsh love spoons, traditional symbols of betrothal intricately carved from single blocks of wood. The museum, housed in a classically designed building which was originally an assize court, preserves the Victorian courthouse intact, complete with prisoner's dock. A second museum, dedicated to the South Wales Borderers, contains a Zulu War Room which commemorates the regiment's heroic defence of Rorke's Drift in 1879.

The grand Church of St John, also known as Brecon Cathedral, really deserves its alternative title. This vast medieval church, which achieved cathedral status in 1923, serves a huge diocese extending as far as Swansea.

 *BRECON, at the junction of the A470 and A40, is 44 miles north of Cardiff.*

BRECON BEACONS MOUNTAIN CENTRE
Powys

On a fine day, the views from the terraces of the Mountain Centre are magnificent. The centre, run by the National Park, is located at an altitude of 1100 ft on Mynydd Illtyd, an open common with panoramic vistas across to the high peaks of the Beacons.

Pen-y-fan, at 2907 ft the loftiest mountain in South Wales, dominates the skyline. Its unusual flat-topped summit crowns a mountain range which is quite unlike any other in Wales. Old red sandstone is the underlying rock, creating a largely

Brecon's market hall, open for business Tuesdays and Fridays

The smooth, green flanks of the Brecon Beacons spread themselves below a series of swooping crests

treeless landscape which rises and falls in a series of gentle, rounded inclines, steep escarpments and razor-sharp ridges.

The Mountain Centre is a mine of information. Maps, models, exhibitions and films introduce visitors to the wealth of outdoor activities on offer in the 520-square-mile National Park,

🚗 *THE CENTRE, located on a minor upland road, is signposted off the A470 at Libanus, 4 miles south-west of Brecon.*

CAERWENT
Gwent

Sleepy Caerwent, skirted by the M4 motorway, is today no more than a village. In Roman times, it was firmly on the map as a large and important city, *Venta Silurum*, 'the market town of the Silures.'

Only by delving into its past can visitors understand the huge stretch of walls, still standing 17 ft high in places, which now defends nothing but green fields. *Venta Silurum* was

founded about A.D. 75 for the local hill tribe, the Silures, as part of the Romans' grand plan to subdue the natives. Quite what the Silures initially made of Roman civilization is anybody's guess, for their new home contained such novelties as public baths, a forum, temple and amphitheatre.

Penhow Castle, two miles to the west, is another history-laden site. Dating from the early 13th century, this fortified manor house claims to be Wales's oldest lived-in castle. As

can be expected from a site which has witnessed so much history and been used as a home for so many centuries, it incorporates a wealth of architectural detail ranging from a Norman bedchamber to a Victorian housekeeper's room.

🚗 *CAERWENT is on the A48 between Chepstow and Newport, accessible from junctions 22 and 24 off the M4 motorway.*

CALDICOT
Gwent

Most visitors to Caldicot come by night, to enjoy the candlelit medieval banquets which are held within the walls of the castle. This is a pity, for this strangely unknown fortress only reveals its true size and splendour to daytime guests.

Caldicot Castle stands in a beautiful country park setting on the edge of an expanding town. Its solid round keep immediately catches the eye. This is the earliest stonework, probably put up by Humphrey de Bohun in the 13th century. Although a site of great antiquity, the castle is largely intact. The 14th-century Great Gatehouse, for example, still sees regular service as the venue for the nightly banquets of dubious 'medieval' authenticity.

The whole castle, snug within its walls, is full of interest. Medieval military architecture merges with Tudor-style half-timbered influences, the castle benefitting from a thorough yet sympathetic restoration in the last century.

Conspicuous amongst the exhibits in the castle museum is the huge figurehead rescued from the *Foudroyant*, Nelson's 'darling child' of a ship that was wrecked in 1897.

🚗 *CALDICOT, on the B4245, is 5 miles south-west of Chepstow, 6 miles east of Newport.*

5

CARREG CENNEN CASTLE
Dyfed

This castle invites superlatives. It has been variously described as 'the most theatrical of British castles' and an 'eagle's nest' fortress. Carreg Cennen, a lonely sentinel, crowns a limestone outcrop in the foothills of the remote Black Mountain. Its battlements are built into a sheer cliff which drops dizzily into the valley below. Weatherbeaten but unbowed, this castle is one of those rare historic sites which evokes the spirit of medieval Wales in an authentic, profound way.

The castle site is an ancient one. Roman coins have been found on the summit of this natural defensive position, which saw much bloody action during the troubled 13th century. A complicated series of fortifications cover the hilltop, which commands breathtaking — though windy — views of the unexplored western corner of the Brecon Beacons National Park. Below the surface, a narrow passageway, cut into the cliff face, leads to a cave beneath the foundations where prehistoric skeletons were unearthed. The mighty 'showpiece' castles of North Wales might be better known. Carreg Cennen is the one which lingers in the memory.

THE CASTLE is located near the village of Trapp, 3 miles south-east of Llandeilo.

CHEPSTOW
Gwent

Most motorists entering Wales by the Severn Bridge and M4 motorway sweep past this charming little town, unaware of its existence. This was not always possible. Chepstow is an historic gateway settlement which once controlled a strategic river crossing into Wales.

The Normans constructed a castle here, on slopes above a great bend in the River Wye. Theirs was no ordinary stronghold, for Chepstow was the first stone-built castle in Britain. Its sturdy walls, on a river cliff above the swirling, muddy-brown waters of the Wye, mark the end of crude earth-and-timber defences and the dawn of a new era in castle construction.

The castle was started shortly after William the Conquerer's victory at Hastings in 1066. Over the years — right up to the 17th century, in fact — Chepstow was improved and added to. As well as being an important first, this fascinating fortress is therefore one of the few sites which spells out in its stonework all the different periods of castle building.

The town of Chepstow grew up on the hillside around the castle, its narrow streets, medieval gate and remnants of town walls providing further evidence of a long history. North of the town, in open, glorious countryside, stands Chepstow Racecourse, the largest in Wales.

CHEPSTOW is located 1½ miles north of Junction 22 on the M4 motorway, directly after the Severn Bridge.

Left: Chepstow Castle, an architectural landmark as Britain's first stone-built fortress

CRICKHOWELL
Powys

The Welsh derivation of the town's name, *Crug Howell* ('Howell's Fort'), refers to the ancient Celtic stronghold on the flat-topped summit of Table Mountain, which looms above the rooftops. Crickhowell still has the air of an old coaching and market town. The Bear Hotel — an historic coaching inn — retains its cobbled courtyard and archway decorated with the words 'Post Horses'. Georgian streets lined with fashionable craft and clothes shops lead down to the River Usk, spanned by a picturesque 13-arched stone bridge.

The long, narrow bridge, put up in the 16th and 17th centuries, continues to carry traffic. St Edmund's Church, dating from the 14th century, is another historic landmark. The church's tall, needle-sharp spire and striking red-tiled roof make it easy to spot. Its porch contains a stone slab which laid down the marital law to 19th-century parishioners in no uncertain terms. Thirty categories of relation, to whom marriage is forbidden, are blacklisted, culminating in wife's sister's daughters!

CRICKHOWELL is on the A40, 6 miles north-west of Abergavenny.

THE GOSPEL PASS
Powys

Few roads make any serious attempts to venture into the largely uninhabited Black Mountains. The Gospel Pass, a bold exception, strikes out due south from Hay-on-Wye, gradually climbing into high country.

The road, a narrow one with airy, panoramic views around almost every bend, runs along the lower slopes of Hay Bluff, a massive shoulder of land rising to 2200 ft. From here, the thin grey strip of tarmac takes advantage of a slight break in the ridge, climbing to a summit of 1778 ft before plunging into the secluded Vale of Ewyas, past Capel-y-ffin, with its little chapel and monastery, to Llanthony Priory.

The Gospel Pass's narrowness and great scenic qualities can also create great traffic congestion, especially on busy summer weekends. At its peaceful best — try to come out-of-season, or at least during mid week in summer — a drive over the Gospel Pass is a stirring experience.

THE GOSPEL PASS leads off the B4350 on the outskirts of Hay-on-Wye.

HAY-ON-WYE
Powys

Anyone interested in books needs no introduction to this small town with a big reputation. At the last count, there were 14 major bookshops here, easily justifying Hay's claim to the title of 'second-hand book capital of the world'.

Businesses which previously sold groceries and hardware have been converted into bookshops. Films are no longer shown at Hay's cinema, the building now stocking a good portion of the million-odd books which are for sale in this town of only one thousand people.

Hay is a paradise for bibliophiles and browsers. Antiquarian books and prints are also sold, together with an excellent selection of new titles often at knock-down, bargain prices.

If visitors can tear themselves away from the miles of book-laden, groaning shelves, they will discover a delightfully unspoilt town of terraced stone cottages, steep streets and an old covered marketplace. The main part of the town is neatly contained between the River Wye, at its foot, and the ruined castle-cum-mansion on a perch above the rooftops.

HAY, on the B4350, is accessible off the A438 north-east of Brecon.

LLANDEILO
Dyfed

The lords of Dinefwr, the ancient rulers of South Wales, presided over their kingdom from Dinefwr Castle, now a romantic ruin veiled amongst trees and ivy on its rocks to the west of the town. The Tywi winds its way along the foot of both castle and town in a rich, green and fertile river valley on which Llandeilo depends for its livelihood.

Llandeilo is an olde-worlde collection of narrow, steep-sided streets lined with little businesses which serve the prosperous farmlands of the Vale of Tywi. From the south the town is approached by a beautifully designed, slender single-span bridge, its 145 ft arch said to be the longest in Wales. A deer herd, arboretum, woodland walks and formal gardens are all contained within the Gelli Aur Country Park, just over four miles south-west of Llandeilo.

LLANDEILO, which can be reached on the A40 and A483, is about 22 miles north of Swansea.

LLANDOVERY
Dyfed

George Borrow, the 19th-century traveller and writer whose classic book, *Wild Wales*, is still in print, described Llandovery as 'the pleasantest little town in which I have halted in the course of my wanderings'. He stayed at the Castle Hotel; those following in his footsteps might wish to know that the four-poster bed in which he slept is still there, in the rechristened 'Borrow Room'.

Llandovery, little changed since Borrow's visit over 100 years ago, continues to delight visitors. It has escaped the blight of modern development and remains a Welsh country town through and through. The ruined castle, a precarious grey shell on a steep earthen tump, overlooks the sheep pens where the weekly livestock markets are held. The town square, with its covered market place, cobbles and clocktower, is charming. And on a hill on the outskirts stands a large church, its presence signalled by a sturdy 13th-century tower, built on the site of a Roman camp.

LLANDOVERY is on the A40, 20 miles west of Brecon at the junction with the A483 and A4069.

LLANGORSE
Powys

Llangorse provides the setting for the largest natural lake in South Wales. The lake, fringed by reed beds and low-lying fields, fills one of the few stretches of flat land in the Brecon Beacons. On a still day, its waters — one mile long by half-a-mile wide — mirror the distinctive summit of Pen-y-fan, the highest peak in the Beacons.

Llangorse village, a short distance from the lake, is a pretty cluster of cottages which grew up around an ancient church and bridge. The Church of St Paulinus, Norman in design, retains part of its original roof. It is named after Paulinus, a 6th-century missionary and tutor to St David, Wales's patron saint, who founded a religious community here.

LLANGORSE, on the B4560, is 6 miles east of Brecon.

LLANTHONY
Gwent

Mountain-locked Llanthony, on the road to nowhere in particular, is not the kind of place visitors tend to stumble on by chance. The hamlet is hidden away in the remote Vale of Ewyas, deep in the Black Mountains.

Religious men in search of solitude founded a monastery here in the early 12th century. In the words of the peripatetic medieval chronicler, Giraldus Cambrensis (Gerald of Wales), no place was more 'truly calculated for religion' than Llanthony. The priory as it now stands, dating from 1175, forms the core of the hamlet. Although 800 years old, the original beauty of this red-stoned ruin survives, aided and abetted by timeless, unchanging surroundings. Its greatest glory is a magnificent avenue of pointed archways framing open hill-sheep country.

Llanthony has captivated many, though for the 19th-century poet, Walter Savage Landor, the outcome was unhappy. He bought the estate with grandiose plans to install himself as the model country gentleman. The locals, however, were unimpressed and Landor left under a cloud in 1813, never to return.

At one time in its history, part of the abandoned priory was used as a shooting box with a licence to sell drink. This explains Llanthony's unique 'pub in the priory' — a tiny hotel-cum-inn, built over the abbot's house, with a deserved reputation for good food and beer.

LLANTHONY can be reached by the B4423 north of Abergavenny or from Hay-on-Wye via the narrow Gospel Pass mountain road.

Llanthony's ruined priory, alone in the tranquil Vale of Ewyas

LLYN-Y-FAN FACH and LLYN-Y-FAN FAWR
Dyfed/Powys

Myth and legend surround this pair of isolated lakes, well and truly off-the-beaten-track in the wilderness of the Black Mountain. Of the two, Llyn-y-Fan Fach is the more accessible. The lake shelters beneath a near vertical escarpment which curves around the shoreline, forming a natural amphitheatre for its black waters.

This gloomily beautiful setting inspired the story of a Lady of the Lake who rose from the waters to marry a farmer. She, and the farm's entire herd of cattle, disappeared into the lake when the farmer struck her three times, though only in play.

The couple are said to have raised sons with remarkable healing powers. Whether by coincidence or not, the Physicians of Myddfai — a village five miles away and the only settlement of note near the lake — were famous, and much in demand, throughout medieval Wales.

Llyn-y-Fan Fach lies beneath the Carmarthen Van, at 2632 ft the highest point in the Black Mountain. A spectacular ridge walk runs through these boggy uplands from one lake to the other.

 THE LAKES should be approached via the hamlet of Llanddeusant, accessible off the A4069 Brynaman to Llangadog road. Park near the waterworks and follow the unmade track.

MONMOUTH
Gwent

A statue of Charles Rolls, of Rolls-Royce fame, stands amongst traditional hotels and coaching inns in Monmouth's tightly-packed main square. Rolls, born at nearby Hendre, is not the only famous figure to have associations with this prosperous old country town. In 1387, Henry V was born in Monmouth Castle — now in ruins, alas, though his statue shares a place in the square with Rolls.

Admiral Lord Nelson's visit of 1802 is remembered at the local museum which contains, amongst other Nelson memorabilia, an outstanding model of his flagship, H.M.S. *Victory*. Place names such as Agincourt Square and Glendower Street reflect Monmouth's involvement in the mainstream of Welsh and English history. The Monnow Bridge is undoubtedly the town's most interesting historic landmark. This 13th-century fortified bridge gateway, the only one of its kind in Britain, still restricts access into the town, its narrow portal proving most effective against the modern motor car.

Nelson journeyed to the 840 ft high summit of The Kymin, one mile east of Monmouth, during his visit to admire the views and the Naval Temple, a monument erected in 1800 to commemorate British victories at sea.

 MONMOUTH stands at the junction of the A40 with the A466, just inside the Welsh border.

RAGLAN
Gwent

All attention here centres on the castle. Raglan is one of Wales's most handsome — even elegant — ruined fortresses. Its grandeur is linked to its status as 'the last medieval castle', for by the time Raglan came to be constructed, castle builders could afford to pay more attention to decoration and less to defence.

This shapely castle belongs mainly to the early 15th century, a product more of social aspiration than military necessity. Sir William ap Thomas, an ambitious royal servant, began work here in 1431. His preoccupations, and those who succeeded him, are clearly evident in Raglan's stately tower and, most of all, the Great Hall, the former splendour of which is hinted at by its finely decorated windows, roof and vast fireplace.

For all its embellishment, Raglan was no weak-walled pushover. This extensive, moated fortress can pride itself in enduring the longest siege of the Civil War.

 RAGLAN is situated on the A40 about half-way between Monmouth and Abergavenny, and 12 miles north-east of Newport.

TALYBONT-ON-USK
Powys

The place name of *Talybont* is a confusingly popular one in Wales. This particular Talybont is located amongst green farmlands on the side of forested slopes in the gentle Vale of Usk.

The river, some distance from the village, is somewhat usurped by a second waterway — the Monmouthshire and Brecon Canal — which flows right through Talybont supported by massive retaining walls. The canal was built between 1799 and 1812 to connect Brecon with Newport and the Severn estuary. Originally, it carried coal, wool and lime. Today, this scenic waterway, navigable for 33 miles through some of the loveliest countryside in the Brecon Beacons National Park, serves a different purpose. It is popular with holiday cruisers, many of which are invariably berthed along the towpath next to Talybont's excellent selection of pubs and inns.

 TALYBONT, on the B4558, is 6 miles south-east of Brecon and 7 miles north-west of Crickhowell.

TINTERN
Gwent

The thick woods and lazily-flowing waters in the Wye Valley between Monmouth and Chepstow have always inspired peace and contemplation. Tintern stands in a particularly tranquil spot. Here, in the 12th century, white-robed Cistercian monks founded a great religious house which was an active community until its dissolution in 1536.

In later centuries, the roofless abbey attracted artists and poets, including William Wordsworth who was inspired to pen his famous sonnet. This evocative, well-preserved ruin still retains much of its original grace and dignity. The abbey's majestic arches, walls and windows point skywards in complete harmony with its sheltered riverside setting.

Tintern itself is a small, scattered settlement in a part of the Wye Valley officially designated as being of 'Outstanding Natural Beauty'.

From the old railway station, now converted into a countryside information centre, waymarked walks lead through the woodlands. Most spectacular of all is the Wyndcliff walk and viewpoint high above the valley two miles to the south.

TINTERN is on the A466 5 miles north of Chepstow, 10 miles south of Monmouth.

TRETOWER COURT AND CASTLE
Powys

This is an interesting two-in-one historic site. A starkly simple round tower, unambiguously military in design and purpose, stands in meadows next to a substantial fortified manor house which must have been a comfortable residence in its time.

Tintern Abbey's soaring arches and sylvan setting have struck a chord with many artists and writers

When the tower, or keep, was put up in the bellicose 12th century, life in Wales was full of threat. The court, in contrast, has all the home comforts of the more settled 14th and 15th centuries. A stone gatehouse leads to a grassy courtyard surrounded by rooms which contain superb examples of late-medieval craftsmanship in stone and wood (the woodwork and timber fittings in the hall and gallery are exceptional).

The court is also notable for its general state of preservation and similarity, in plan, to the colleges of Oxford and Cambridge. Tretower was the home of Henry Vaughan, the celebrated 17th-century metaphysical poet who is buried at nearby Llansantffraed Church.

🚗 *TRETOWER is near the junction of the A40 and A479, 9 miles northwest of Abergavenny.*

USK
Gwent

Usk takes its name from the mighty river that marks the western boundary of this compact little town located in quiet and rural border country. To the Romans, who built an important fortress here, it was known as *Burrium*. One thousand years later, the Normans arrived and founded a castle on the hill above the river. More substantial stone defences were built in later centuries, the 14th-century gatehouse now serving as a family house for a castle that is in private ownership and not normally open to the public.

Usk relies on its river for more than its name. The inns, tackle shops and fishing hotels ranged around the spacious town square benefit from the excellent salmon and trout waters.

🚗 *USK stands at the junction of the A472 and A471 just off the A499, 9 miles north of Newport.*

WHITE CASTLE
Gwent

This castle should not really be viewed in isolation. Together with two others — Grosmont and Skenfrith — it formed a triangle of strongholds which plugged a gap in a weak section of the troublesome border country between England and Wales.

The 'Three Castles of Gwent' were built in stone largely in the 13th and 14th centuries on foundations of earlier fortifications. White Castle, so called because of the white plaster which originally covered its walls, must have been a stunning sight indeed in its prime. The placid rural

The smooth, deep waters of the River Usk are rich in salmon and trout

retreat of Skenfrith in the once-bloody borderlands is noted for its powerful round tower and ring of curtain walls. French influences at Grosmont extend beyond the style of military architecture employed to the name itself, *gros mont* being a Gallic equivalent to 'big hill'.

THE 'THREE CASTLES' *are within 5 miles of each other near the Wales/England border in the countryside to the north-east of Abergavenny.*

WOLVESNEWTON
Gwent

This scattered hamlet, in peaceful rolling countryside between the Vales of Usk and Wye, is the home of the Model Farm Folk Collection and Craft Centre. The farm itself is a rather special one: it is dominated by a unique, cross-shaped barn, built by the Duke of Beaufort at the end of the 18th century.

This cruciform barn now houses a folk collection which reflects agricultural and domestic life over the last one hundred years or so, mainly from Queen Victoria's time to the coronation of Elizabeth II. The farm site also contains a mill gallery of changing exhibitions and craft workshops where the traditional skills of the potter and corn dolly maker can be seen.

WOLVESNEWTON, *10 miles north-west of Chepstow, can be reached from the east via Devauden* on the B4293 and via Llangwm, on the B4235, from the west.

YSTRADFELLTE
Powys

This tiny hamlet — a church, whitewashed pub, post office and handful of houses — is better known than its size suggests. Its name is synonymous with the distinctive limestone scenery which occurs along the southern rim of the Brecon Beacons National Park.

Unlike the wide and open spaces in the rest of the park, the waterfall country around Ystradfellte consists of thickly wooded gorges carved deep into the landscape and riddled with caves and pot-holes. Just south of the hamlet, the River Mellte completely disappears for one-quarter of a mile as it is swallowed up by the gaping Porth-yr-Ogof cavern.

The river reappears only to tumble, a mile further on, down a series of spectacular waterfalls in a shady, steep-sided valley. The most famous waterfall of all is on the River Hepste, a tributary of the Mellte. This is Sgwd-yr-Eira ('The Spout of Snow'), which overhangs to such an extent that a footpath passes behind it.

YSTRADFELLTE *is on a minor road off the A4059, approximately 12 miles north-west of Merthyr Tydfil.*

The cascading River Mellte in Ystradfellte's 'waterfall country'

The Romans in Wales

The Romans' self-confident boast, 'Veni, Vidi, Vici' ('I came, I saw, I conquered') might have applied elsewhere in their empire. In Wales, victory was never unequivocal, conquest never complete.

Difficult highland terrain populated by non-cooperative, if not downright intransigent Celtic tribes created problems which they never encountered in the intensively Romanized south and east of Britain. Some kind of wary co-existence was eventually achieved — after all, the Romans remained in Wales for over 300 years — though Roman might was largely confined to the more manageable lowland areas of Wales.

The Romans invaded Britain in A.D. 43. Tentative expeditions into Wales, possibly inspired by the lure of Welsh gold, prepared the ground for an arrival in strength in A.D. 74. Those wishing to follow in the Romans' footsteps should start, as they did, at Caerleon, where a powerful base was constructed for the crack Second Augustan Legion.

At nearby Caerwent, they created a city which introduced Roman notions of civilization to the natives. They also set about building a network of roads which linked their two main bases at Caerleon and Chester with a series of lesser forts. And at Pumpsaint, deep in the hills, they found what they had been looking for — gold.

Tracking down traces of these ambitious empire builders can be a tantalising process. Their straight-as-a-dye, well engineered

road systems outlive them still. In some cases — across Gelligaer Common north of Caerphilly, for example — modern road builders have simply followed old Roman routes. In others, the original trackways remain, charting typically direct and uncompromising courses across inhospitable moorland. And, scattered throughout Wales, grassy hummocks and fragmentary remains indicate the existence of Roman outposts (*Y Gaer*, their fort near Brecon, is one such site).

The Roman hold on Wales, although never complete, left its mark — and brought its benefits. Their departure, at the end of the 4th century, left Wales unprotected against the Saxons, Picts and Irish Goidel tribes. The end of the empire for Rome meant the beginning of a Dark Age for Wales.

Foundations of Roman houses at Caerwent

Caerleon amphitheatre

South Wales & Gower

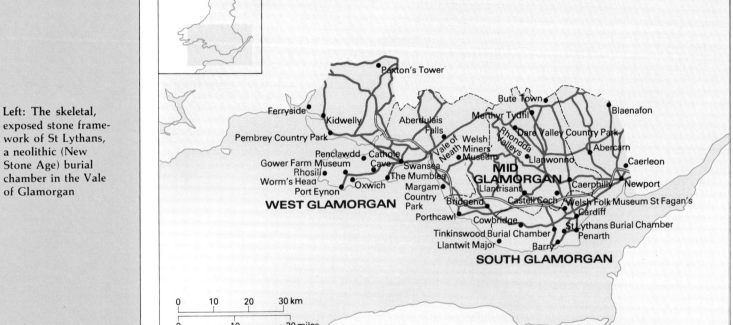

Left: The skeletal, exposed stone framework of St Lythans, a neolithic (New Stone Age) burial chamber in the Vale of Glamorgan

Map labels: Paxton's Tower, Ferryside, Kidwelly, Pembrey Country Park, Penclawdd, Gower Farm Museum, Rhosili, Worm's Head, Port Eynon, Oxwich, Aberdulais Falls, Cathole Cave, Swansea, The Mumbles, Margam Country Park, Bridgend, Porthcawl, Cowbridge, Tinkinswood Burial Chamber, Llantwit Major, Vale of Neath, Welsh Miners' Museum, Bute Town, Merthyr Tydfil, Rhondda Valleys, Dare Valley Country Park, Llanwonno, Llantrisant, Castell Coch, Barry, Blaenafon, Abercarn, Caerleon, Newport, Caerphilly, Welsh Folk Museum St Fagan's, Cardiff, St Lythans Burial Chamber, Penarth

WEST GLAMORGAN **MID GLAMORGAN** **SOUTH GLAMORGAN**

Scale: 0 10 20 30 km
0 10 20 miles

VISITORS WHO WANDER amongst the Neo-Classical buildings of dazzling white Portland stone in Cardiff's Civic Centre may have cause to review their opinions about South Wales. Cardiff, as they will discover, is anything but a lacklustre coal port. Along the cliff-backed Glamorgan coast, Swansea's prestigious new Maritime Quarter is transforming the old waterfront. And the valleys of South Wales, contrary to popular opinion, no longer bristle with pit headgear.

South Wales, misrepresented in the past, should not be ignored in the present. Its powerful personality, a consequence of the dynamic role it played during the Industrial Revolution, demands attention — as do its surprising and dramatic scenic qualities.

Country parks and forests now account for much more landscape than coalmines. Late 20th-century visitors are reminded of the 'good old, bad old days' of the 19th century mainly through sites specially preserved for their industrial heritage. No one claims that all of the old scars have disappeared. Yet it is easier, nowadays, to begin to comprehend the 18th-century, pre-industrial view of the valleys.

Further west, the scenic qualities of the Gower coast are beyond dispute. This stubby peninsula, 20 miles long, was declared Britain's first official 'Area of Outstanding Natural Beauty' in 1956. Its protected shoreline, a succession of towering sea-cliffs and sandy bays in the south, leads to lonely salt-marsh along the Loughor estuary.

15

ABERDULAIS FALLS
West Glamorgan

Aberdulais is one of those rare sites which manages to marry two apparently irreconcilable bedfellows — great natural beauty and industrial exploitation. The former comes from its setting. Here, in a tree-shrouded gorge, the waters of the Dulais tumble over mossy ledges and through narrow, rocky channels. By the late 18th century, this romantically gloomy spot was attracting artists and writers from far and wide, including the incomparable J.M.W. Turner whose sketchbooks contain a large number of drawings of the falls.

A jumble of ruined masonry, currently being restored by the National Trust, mingles with the woods along the banks of the falls, from which power was harnessed by water-wheel to drive the bellows of a pioneering smelting works. This is an important industrial site, one of the earliest in South Wales, which started life in 1584 as a copper works, later moving to iron and tin.

🚗 *ABERDULAIS is at the junction of the A465 and A4109 in the Vale of Neath, about 7 miles north-east of Swansea.*

BARRY AND PENARTH
South Glamorgan

This pair of coastal towns, kept apart by the headlands at Lavernock, have little in common even though they share the same Victorian roots.

Barry grew up in the 1880s, a consequence of the increasing number of frustrations and holdups at Cardiff docks. The docklands founded here by coalowner David Davies were soon booming, and in 1913 Barry exported a record-breaking 11 million tons of coal hewn from the neighbouring valleys.

Barry Island, a popular and lively seaside resort, is an island no more, thanks to the dockland developments which bonded it to the mainland. Barry's quieter side resides along The Knap, where a long, steeply-shelving pebble beach leads to a rocky coastline of white limestone cliffs. Porthkerry Country Park, directly landward from these cliffs, is a spacious swathe of grassland, oak and ash wood spanned by an elegant 18-arched railway viaduct.

Penarth was much favoured by Cardiff's prosperous 19th-century coalowners and shipping magnates. Their palatial homes overlook a promenade — complete with ornate pier and sea-front gardens — that still retains the genteel character of a fashionable Victorian watering hole. Penarth's Turner House Art Gallery, part of the National Museum of Wales, exhibits both classical and modern works.

🚗 *BARRY AND PENARTH, a few miles south-west of Cardiff, can be reached by the A4055 and A4160 from the city.*

BEAUPRE CASTLE
South Glamorgan

Beaupre — pronounced 'Bewper' and also known as Old Beaupre — is a reclusive historic site. Visitors have to embark on a longish, though most pleasant, stroll across rolling river meadows to reach its handsome walls.

The castle is something of a hybrid, an Elizabethan mansion more than a medieval fortress. Its walls, though strong and tall, enclose what is, in essence, a substantial home which displays many stylish features.

Large, mullioned windows add light to the courtyard. Beaupre's outstanding decorative features are at the entrance to, and within, this courtyard. An outer porch, dated 1586, bears the arms of the Bassetts (the family intimately linked with Beaupre's history since medieval times) and their motto (in Welsh), 'Better Death than Shame'. The inner porch is grander still, a three-tiered affair carved in classical style from a sandy stone.

🚗 *BEAUPRE CASTLE is approximately 1 mile south-west of St Hillary, a village accessible off the A48 just east of Cowbridge.*

BLAENAFON
Gwent

On the face of it, Blaenafon is a most unlikely candidate for inclusion within these pages. Yet thousands of visitors now make their way each year to this rather unkempt old valley town, attracted by the presence of the Big Pit Mining Museum.

The pit headgear on the bare hillside above the town identifies a site that is unique in Britain. Until 1980, Big Pit was a working coalmine. In 1983 it re-opened as a living museum which gives visitors first-hand experience of what life was really like for generations of South Wales miners.

Groups of the public, kitted out in safety helmets, cap lamps and battery belts descend 300 ft by miners' cage to pit bottom for a conducted tour of the old underground workings. On the surface, too, an air of authenticity prevails. Everything has been left very much as it was in the pithead baths, working forge, colliery workshops and engine house.

For anyone professing an understanding of the old South Wales industrial communities, a visit to Blaenafon is obligatory — doubly so, since both iron and coal played their parts here. Blaenafon Ironworks, also open to the public, contains some of

the finest surviving late 18th-century blast furnaces in Europe, an impressive water balance tower and the ruins of ironworkers' cottages.

🚗 *BLAENAFON is on the A4043 north of Newport and B4246 south-west of Abergavenny.*

At Blaenafon visitors with a strong sense of history can make their way to the Big Pit Mining Museum and descend to pit bottom in a cramped miners' cage, after being kitted out with safety helmets, cap lamps and battery belts

BRIDGEND
Mid Glamorgan

This large settlement is mentioned on the strength of what can be seen around and about, as opposed to in the town itself.

The priory church at Ewenny, just over one mile to the south, is delightful. The church, which contains fine Norman work, stands on a quiet riverbank amongst the ruins of a Benedictine priory, founded in the 12th century, amid an atmosphere of cool tranquillity.

Religious and military influences appear to have been at work here. Parts of the site — the tower in particular — are decidedly robust in their architecture, making this one of the best defended churches in to survive Britain.

Coity Castle, two miles north-east of Bridgend, is military pure and simple. Originally an earth-and-timber Norman stronghold, Coity was later rebuilt in stone. Further remodelling and strengthening in the 14th century was prescient, allowing the castle to withstand a long siege during the Welsh uprising in the early 15th century.

🚗 *BRIDGEND, at the junction of the A48, A473, A4061 and A4063 is 20 miles west of Cardiff.*

BUTE TOWN
Mid Glamorgan

Bute Town is an oddity. For a start, it is a tiny, self-contained village, not a town. More important still, Bute Town defies all the conventions of architecture in the South Wales valleys. The traditional and typical view of terraced housing, one row stacked above the next along the valley slopes, is turned completely on its head at this early model village, built around 1802 by an altruistic local ironmaster to house his workers.

Bute Town's warm-stoned houses — some three storeys high — and wide streets, laid out to an orderly, neat plan, are quite unlike anything else in South Wales. The village remains faithful to its original looks, having benefitted from sympathetic restoration during 1975's European Architectural Heritage Year.

🚗 *BUTE TOWN, just north of Rhymney, is accessible off the A465 'Heads of the Valleys' road 4 miles east of Merthyr Tydfil.*

CAERLEON
Gwent

Motorists approaching Newport on the M4 motorway into Wales are mostly unaware that they are speeding past one of the most important Roman sites in Britain. In Roman times, all roads led into Caerleon — or, as it was known then, *Isca.* Together with Chester and York, Caerleon was one of only three fortresses in Britain built to accommodate legionary soldiers, the crack troops of the Roman army.

From A.D. 74, this grassy spot by a bend in the river was the home of the 6000-strong Second Augustan Legion. Caerleon, amongst the largest Roman military sites in northern Europe, was no rough-and-ready army camp. A legionary baths complex has recently been excavated, revealing part of a large, multi-purpose range of buildings — the Roman equivalent to today's sports and leisure centre. Hot and cold baths could be taken here in carefully controlled temperatures. The foundations of an open-air swimming pool are clearly visible next to areas where sporting and non-athletic pastimes (including eating, drinking and gambling) could be pursued or indulged.

Another, darker form of entertainment took place at Caerleon's showpiece Roman site. In its famous, well-preserved amphitheatre thousands of excited spectators once witnessed grim blood sports including gladiatorial combat and animal baiting.

In fields just north of the amphitheatre, the orderly foundations of the soldier's barracks have also been excavated and are on view.

CAERLEON, on the B4236, can be reached from junctions 24 and 25 off the M4 motorway.

CAERPHILLY
Mid Glamorgan

Caerphilly's reputation is in a state of flux. The eponymous cheese, which turned this town into a household name, is no longer made here. Instead, Caerphilly is becoming increasingly well-known on the strength of its quite remarkable castle, now ranked as one of Europe's greatest surviving medieval fortresses.

Probably because of its setting within an unpretentious and otherwise unremarkable valley town, only recently has Caerphilly Castle's true status been generally appreciated. In the hierarchy of British castles, 30-acre Caerphilly stands near the top: only at Dover, and possibly Windsor, is it equalled in size.

The Norman lord, Gilbert de Clare, wary of the native Welsh, commenced serious work on the castle in the 1270s. He created a mighty 'stone and water' system of concentric defences built up, barrier after barrier, from a central core like the layers of an onion. His grey-green walls and powerful gatehouse still stand to their full height above the waters of the moat. The only weak note is struck by a tipsy ruined tower on the site, which manages to out-lean even the world-famous example at Pisa.

CAERPHILLY, on the junction of the A469 and A468, is 8 miles north of Cardiff.

Under its winter skies Caerphilly looks the part as 'the sleeping giant of British castles'. Historians are already aware of its status as one of the great sites of the medieval western world. The castle, strangely unknown, is only now beginning to attract the public attention it rightly deserves

CARDIFF
South Glamorgan

Wales's capital city, population 285,000, began life as a Roman camp, laying the foundations to its present status in the boom-town years of the 19th century. Cardiff's 2000-year history is epitomised in one edifice — its huge castle, standing tall in the busy heart of the city.

The castle is a unique three-in-one historic site, retaining sections of original Roman walls and a well-preserved Norman keep alongside the lavish, no-expense-spared restoration work carried out in Victorian times. As it now stands, the castle is a testament to the phenomenal 19th-century

growth of Cardiff from humble sea-town into one of the world's premier coal-exporting ports.

Vast fortunes were made in Cardiff's docklands, largely by the Bute family. The Third Marquess poured much of his wealth into the re-birth of Cardiff Castle, enlisting the services of the outstanding — albeit eccentric — Victorian architect, William Burges.

From 1868, Burges's 'strange genius' was allowed full rein. He created an opulent, extravagant mansion which flaunts an eclectic range of decorative influences ranging from ancient Greece to the Arabian Nights, all executed with a romantic, mock-medieval flourish.

Sobriety and dignity reign a stone's throw away, at the Civic Centre. The 194-ft dome of the City Hall fronts a collection of Neo-Classical official buildings dating from the turn of the century. Built of white Portland stone and set amongst beautiful parklands and wide, tree-lined avenues, Cardiff's Civic Centre has been rated — along with Washington and New Delhi — as one of the world's most elegant examples of civic architecture.

The cavernous Museum of Wales, one of its buildings, contains an encyclopaedic range of exhibits spanning pre-history and the Industrial Revolution, together with a prized collection of French Impressionist

paintings. Another familiar landmark is the National Stadium (better known, perhaps, as Cardiff Arms Park), the shrine of Welsh rugby. The stadium stands next to the shopping centre where attractive 19th-century features — canopied arcades and a traditional fresh foods market — integrate well with modern pedestrian precincts and the new St David's Centre.

Llandaff, in the western suburbs, is a 'village within a city'. The old village green, next to the soaring twin towers of Llandaff Cathedral, helps it retain its village atmosphere. The cathedral, standing on the site of an important 6th-century religious community, was badly damaged during

20 **William Burges's ornate decoration in Cardiff Castle**

Llandaff Cathedral with its modern sculpture

the last war. Part of its restoration included an uncompromisingly modernistic sculpture by Sir Jacob Epstein, *Christ in Majesty*, which dominates the cathedral interior and is still a source of controversy amongst traditionalists.

🚗 *CARDIFF, accessible off the M4 motorway, is 27 miles from the Severn Bridge.*

CASTELL COCH
South Glamorgan

Castell Coch, 'The Red Castle', leaps straight off the pages of a fairy story or the frames of a Disney movie. Its needle-sharp conical towers prick the skies from their perch on a wooden gorge which guards the northern approach to Cardiff.

A mere 100 years old, this enchanting little castle is a Victorian creation, built as a companion piece to Cardiff Castle for the fabulously wealthy Marquess of Bute. Like its big brother, Castell Coch is a decorative extravaganza. Its rooms are laden with liberal quantities of visual detail depicting Aesop's Fables, figures from Greek mythology, and a Noah's Ark of animals, birds and butterflies.

Purists outraged by Castell Coch's free-ranging excesses can take some comfort in the fact that it at least occupies the site of a genuine medieval stronghold.

🚗 *THE CASTLE, at Tongwynlais off the A470, is 5 miles north-west of Cardiff's city centre.*

Castell Coch — a castle fit for Sleeping Beauty, full of romance

COWBRIDGE
South Glamorgan

This prosperous town — countrified rather than pure country — has become a popular place to live for those who work elsewhere, often in Cardiff, only a short car journey away. Nevertheless, Cowbridge still lives up to its historic status as the 'Capital of the Vale of Glamorgan'.

A long main street, now by-passed by through traffic, is lined with a classy and cosmopolitan collection of shops, inns and restaurants. Cowbridge, possibly of Roman origin, was a fully-fledged market town as long ago as the 11th century. Vestiges of the past can be seen to the south of the main street, where fragmentary remains of the medieval town walls and a well-preserved gateway survive. Other old buildings of note include the Tudor-style school and handsome Town Hall.

COWBRIDGE, *just off the A48, is 12 miles west of Cardiff.*

CWMCARN SCENIC FOREST DRIVE
Gwent

The conifer-clad hills which loom above the valley community of Abercarn can be explored in a most unorthodox fashion. Under normal circumstances, cars are prohibited from using the loose-surfaced roads which run through Forestry Commission plantations. Not so at Cwmcarn, where a seven-mile route is open to the public as a scenic forest drive.

The drive weaves its way between the trees from valley floor to mountain top, with stopping-off places for picnic sites and waymarked forest walks. In its upper reaches, the road skirts the 1374-ft summit of Twm Barlwm, an ancient hill-fort which preserves its earthwork defences. On a clear day, views from the top are spectacular in the extreme. To the north, the distinctive silhouettes of the Brecon Beacons dominate the horizon. Southwards, Newport spreads itself out between the hills of the South Wales valleys and waters of the Severn estuary.

ABERCARN *is on the A467, 8 miles north-west of Newport.'*

DARE VALLEY COUNTRY PARK
Mid Glamorgan

Visitors to this country park find it difficult to accept that it stands on the site of old collieries and coal-tips. They have to look long and hard indeed for any tell-tale signs of the Industrial Revolution amongst the swathes of grassland, forests, streams and lakesides which now adorn the valley slopes above the town of Aberdare.

Dare Valley is a prime example of what has been achieved, in terms of environmental improvement, in the South Wales valleys. Established in 1972 as Wales's first country park, the Dare Valley has erased from the 20th century the scars of the 19th. Half-a-dozen old colliery workings and countless coal-tips were completely removed in an ambitious landscaping exercise which involved the planting of 20,000 trees and the creation of a scenic cascade and fishing lake.

THE COUNTRY PARK *is at Aberdare, on the A4059, about 24 miles north-west of Cardiff.*

DYFFRYN GARDENS
South Glamorgan

These gardens bring a splash of colour to the pervading greenery of the pastoral Vale of Glamorgan. Dyffryn is especially proud of its seasonal bedding displays, rose garden, large herbaceous borders, ponds and individually designed smaller gardens — the Italian Terrace is delightful — all contained within a 50-acre landscaped site.

Various hot houses provide an opportunity to see tropical and sub-tropical species, including palms, orchids, cacti, banana and pineapple plants. The gardens are laid out around Dyffryn House (not open to the public). Built in 1893 in a grand and affluent style, its regal facade reflects the tremendous fortunes which were made from the coal mining industries of South Wales.

DYFFRYN GARDENS *are on a minor road south of St Nicholas, a village on the A48 6 miles west of Cardiff.*

FERRYSIDE
Dyfed

The banks of the Tywi estuary are undeservedly unknown. Forgotten Ferryside is a charming village which displays only faint traces of recognition by the outside world — there is a sailing club here, and the small, pebbly beach sometimes sees visitors.

Tregoning Hill, a National Trust property, stands just south of the village. The views from the hillside are splendid, overlooking the silvery junction of three river systems — the Tywi, Taf and Gwendraeth — and the rich green headlands above Llanstephan, topped by dramatic, ragged castle ruins.

Tucked away below Tregoning Hill is the ancient, ivy-covered Church of St Ishmael's and the lost village of Hawton, said to have been drowned in a great storm which occurred in the 17th century.

FERRYSIDE, *accessible by minor road off the A484, is approximately 10 miles south of Carmarthen.*

GOWER FARM MUSEUM
West Glamorgan

All attention on Gower focusses on the coastline. This museum attempts to redress the balance by introducing visitors to the countryside — specifically, the long history of farming, and farming people, on the Gower peninsula.

The museum's main theme — how people have lived and farmed on Gower in the past 100 years — is told through the eyes of one family, the Watters. Their household goods, farm machinery, butter-making equipment, old documents and family photographs help build up a picture of life on the peninsula before the advent of the tractor and the motor car. Interestingly, the museum also reflects on the relatively recent arrival of visitors from the outside world, for when the Watters were farming here 100 years ago, their peninsula was regarded as a strange, remote backwater.

Most of the exhibits are housed in 17th-century agricultural buildings. This rambling, informal — and informative-museum is one of the surprising number of places to vist away from Gower's magnet-like coast. The pleasant countryside immediately around the museum can be explored via a number of farm trails intended to give walkers an idea of modern methods employed in the surrounding farmlands.

THE MUSEUM *is just over 1 mile west of Reynoldston on a minor road off the A4118 near the hamlet of Knelston.*

Kidwelly Castle, remarkably intact, is an awesome sight. Its twin-towered gatehouse butts into the sky three storeys tall, dominating the surrounding Dyfed countryside

KIDWELLY
Dyfed

Medieval Wales confronts the Industrial Revolution at this friendly sea-town on the Gwendraeth estuary. Kidwelly is dominated by its old stone castle, an outstanding example of the concentric 'walls within walls' system of defence. The castle stands its ground above the rooftops on a slope commanding the estuary, a strategic site carefully chosen so that it could be supplied with food and ammunition by sea if cut off by land. The fortress's original strength prevails even today, thanks to its remarkable state of preservation — especially the twin-towered Great Gatehouse, which stands, three storeys tall, above everything else.

In the 18th century, Kidwelly was in the forefront of tin-plate production in Britain. A 164 ft-high chimneystack, on the outskirts of town, marks the site of its pioneering tin-plate works, now open to the public as the Kidwelly Industrial Museum.

KIDWELLY, at the junction of the A484 and B4308, is 10 miles south of Carmarthen.

LANGLAND AND CASWELL BAYS
West Glamorgan

This pair of perfectly shaped bays shelter amongst breaks in the cliffs at the southern entrance to the unspoilt Gower Peninsula. The beach at Langland Bay lies beneath rocky headlands in a sunny, south-facing position. One of the many spectacular cliff-walks along the Gower coast links Langland to Caswell Bay.

Caswell, 'the jewel of Gower', is a crescent of sand scooped out beneath profusely wooded hillsides. Footpaths penetrate the dense Bishop's

Wood, a nature reserve in a dry valley leading away from the beach. West of Caswell, another path strikes out over the cliffs to the secluded old smugglers' haunt of Brandy Cove.

🚗 *LANGLAND and Caswell Bays can be reached by the B4593, off the A4067 south-west of Swansea.*

LLANTRISANT
Mid Glamorgan

Attention here centres on 'old' Llantrisant up on the hill — not the new housing developments which sprawl around the original town — and the iconoclastic figure of Dr William Price. A statue of Dr Price, resplendent in his fox-skin head-dress, stands amongst the streets in the Bull Ring.

Dr Price (1800-1893) was even more provocative in attitude than appearance. Today, the causes he espoused — nudism, vegetarianism, free love and radical politics — are familiar enough. Straight-laced Victorian society was outraged by them.

His greatest *cause célèbre* occurred in 1884, when he attempted to cremate his illegitimate son, Iesu Grist (Jesus Christ), who had died in infancy, on Llantrisant Common. In the ensuing furore, Dr Price was arrested, tried and acquitted of any crime, as a result of which cremation became legal in Britain.

Dr Price's ghostly presence tends to eclipse anything else in Llantrisant, though it should be mentioned that the ancient town has a fine church, Norman in origin, ivy-covered castle remains and — on the outskirts — the modern Royal Mint complex.

🚗 *LLANTRISANT, on the junction of the A4119 and A473, is 10 miles north-west of Cardiff.*

Left: Caswell, one of the loveliest of Gower's many bays

LLANTWIT MAJOR
South Glamorgan

This pretty little town in the prosperous, pastoral Vale of Glamorgan served as a springboard for Welsh civilization. The sheltered hollow beneath Llantwit Major's narrow, crooked streets was a great religious and educational centre, founded around A.D. 500 by St Illtud, an influential early Christian figure.

St David, Wales's patron saint, studied here in a monastic settlement now occupied by the impressive Church of St Illtud. Like St David's Cathedral, this seminal religious centre stands close to, but invisible from, the sea. St Illtud's grand, cathedral-like dimensions are also reminiscent of St David's. It is, in fact, two churches in one — an earlier Norman and late 13th-century church combined. Painted wall frescos and a fine collection of inscribed Celtic crosses and pillars are amongst its wealth of treasures.

The town's medieval streets are also well endowed with historic buildings, including the Old Swan Inn, Town Hall and stone gabled Ty Mawr ('Great House') on the outskirts.

🚗 *LLANTWIT MAJOR, on the junction of the B4265 and B4270, is approximately 15 miles south-west of Cardiff.*

LLANWONNO
Mid Glamorgan

An old church, a rambling churchyard, a pub that looks too large for its location and a row of cottages are all that make up the hamlet of Llanwonno, standing over 1000 ft high in the hills between the Rhondda and Cynon Valleys.

Those who are sceptical of the scenic qualities on display within this part of South Wales should visit Llanwonno. Its steep approach roads command wonderful views across and into the severe-sided valleys before entering an extensive conifer woodland — the St Gwynno Forest — which completely surrounds the hamlet.

Llanwonno was the home of Guto Nyth Bran, the 18th-century long-distance runner who, according to legend, ran across the mountain to fetch yeast in the time that it took for his mother to bring a kettle of water to the boil.

🚗 *LLANWONNO is accessible by minor roads from Pontypridd (5 miles to the south-east), Ferndale (in the Rhondda Valleys) and Mountain Ash (in the Cynon Valley).*

A Celtic wheel-head cross from Llantwit Major's fine collection

MARGAM COUNTRY PARK
West Glamorgan

Although within shouting distance of the M4 motorway and the Port Talbot-Margam industrial sprawl, this country park is a model of peace and tranquillity. The park — all 850 acres of it — shuts itself off most effectively from the outside world. Fallow deer can usually be seen grazing on its open grassland, which rises up into bracken-covered slopes crowned by an Iron Age hill-fort.

The park is based around a ruined 19th-century castle built in haunting Tudor-Gothic style. Margam's great architectural masterpiece is thankfully well preserved. This is the mid-18th-century orangery, an elegant, well-proportioned building with 27 tall windows in its 327-ft length, built to accommodate orange, lemon and citrus trees.

Twentieth-century art is represented here in the form of an imaginative Sculpture Park, featuring work by internationally famous sculptors. The remains of what was once the largest monastic house in Wales can also be seen, together with early Christian memorial stones.
🚗 *MARGAM COUNTRY PARK is accessible off the A48.*

MERTHYR TYDFIL
Mid Glamorgan

In the tumultuous 19th century, Merthyr Tydfil was the iron-and-steel-producing capital of the world. Today, most of old Merthyr has been redeveloped.

Cyfarthfa Castle is the most conspicuous reminder of Merthyr's heyday. This large Gothic mansion, built by the all-powerful Crawshay iron-masters in 1824, stands imperiously on a hillside amongst pleasant, wooded parkland. A more plaintive — and certainly more telling — monument to this stern family can be seen at Vaynor Church, where Robert Thompson Crawshay's grave bears the simple plea 'God Forgive Me'.

The castle houses an immaculate museum filled with a delightful range of exhibits. Particularly intriguing is the model of Richard Trevithick's steam locomotive, which ran along a tramroad from Merthyr a full 20 years before Stephenson's more famous 'Rocket'. Steam power has now returned to Merthyr in the form of the narrow-gauge Brecon Mountain Railway, which follows a scenic route to a lakeside terminus in the foothills of Brecon Beacons.
🚗 *MERTHYR, at the junction of the A470 and A465, is 25 miles north of Cardiff.*

Merthyr's Cyfarthfa Castle, built with the wealth generated by iron and the Industrial Revolution

THE MUMBLES
West Glamorgan

This strangely-titled place — no one seems to know the origin of its name — is also a strange mixture of sailing centre-cum-seaside resort-cum-

suburb of Swansea. The Mumbles is tucked snugly away along the sheltered western shore of Swansea Bay at the gateway to the Gower Peninsula. Hotels, guesthouses, boat parks and pubs — the Antelope Hotel and Mermaid were favourite ports of call for the young Dylan Thomas — line a seafront which leads to Mumbles Head.

The views across Swansea Bay from the pier and lighthouse on this rocky promontory are matched by those from Oystermouth Castle. Dating from 1280, this splendid old fortification stands to its original height on a grassy knoll above the rooftops.

🚗 *THE MUMBLES is on the B4433, accessible off the A4067 5 miles south-west of Swansea.*

NEWPORT
Gwent

Modern Newport, the largest town in the county of Gwent, does not look as though it was founded way back in the 6th century. There is, however, a surprising amount of history scattered around the town. The riverside towers of Newport Castle now appear a little lost, marooned amongst busy shops, road systems and a new multi-million pound leisure centre. This medieval castle replaced an earlier one which stood on Stow Hill beside St Woolos's Cathedral.

The hilltop cathedral, occupying a religious site as old as the town itself, is a fine affair noteworthy for its Norman work. Newport's sometimes turbulent history is recalled at the excellent Museum and Art Gallery — though the best paintings of all are in the Civic Centre, decorated by a striking series of heroic murals.

Newport's skyline is dominated by its unusual Edwardian Transporter Bridge (currently closed, alas), a monumental web of girders straddling the waters of the River Usk. Another form of transportation — the inland waterways of the 19th century — is the basis for the exhibitions at the 14 Locks Canal Centre, named after a massive staircase of locks on the outskirts of town.

Fourteen locks stands near to Newport's most significant historic site. The town's rapid expansion as a port serving the 19th-century iron and coal industries of the South Wales valleys is embodied in the fabric of Tredegar House. This magnificent red-bricked Restoration mansion, built between 1664 and 1672, really came of age in the mid 19th century thanks to the wealth of Newport's docklands. Its gilded, opulent interior is complemented by superb surroundings, now a 90-acre country park.

🚗 *NEWPORT, accessible off the M4 motorway, is 11 miles from Cardiff.*

OXWICH
West Glamorgan

The variety of landscape and coastline at Oxwich is remarkable. This undeveloped little coastal hamlet's long and accommodating beach is just the start of the story. The beach is backed by the sand dunes of Oxwich Burrows which, in turn, border a large, watery area of marsh and reed beds. This entire low-lying area is protected by a craggy headland, its slopes covered by a thick blanket of oak and ash woods leading to Oxwich Point.

Little wonder, then, that Oxwich, with its unusually wide range of wildlife habitats, has become a nature reserve. Provision is also made for the public, thanks to a helpful information centre and series of waymarked walks.

Oxwich is, quite understandably, mainly popular for its sands. Oxwich Bay sweeps along for well over a mile, ending at the lovely — but somewhat inaccessible — Three Cliffs Bay, a famous Gower beauty spot. The tiny 13th-century Church of St Illtyd, barely visible in the woods beyond the beach, stands beneath a steep slope crowned by Oxwich Castle, a 16th-century manor house currently under restoration. A little way inland, and visible from the surrounding high ground, are two more castles — the 'Old' and 'New' Penrice Castles — in a private estate.

🚗 *OXWICH is accessible off the A4118 approximately 13 miles west of Swansea.*

PARC LE BREOS BURIAL CHAMBER AND CATHOLE CAVE
West Glamorgan

The secluded, wooded valley running north-west from Parkmill can only be explored on foot. The walk is well worth it, not only for the tranquil surroundings but also for this pair of prehistoric sites which hide themselves away here.

Gower is dotted with evidence of prehistoric settlement, none more conclusive than Parc le Breos which stands in open grassland encircled by thick woods. This stone tomb — very well preserved considering its age — was used for the communal burial of the dead. Although at least 4000 years old, it is a relative newcomer in comparison to Cathole Cave, located in the hillside further along the valley. Mammoth and woolly rhinocerous bones have been found here, in a cave inhabited by man 10,000 years ago towards the end of the Ice Age.

🚗 *PARKMILL, on the A4118, is about 8 miles west of Swansea.*

PAXTON'S TOWER
Dyfed

This tower is pure folly. Put up by Sir William Paxton in the early 19th century, it fulfills no other purpose than to commemorate Lord Nelson.

Its castellated walls, on the crest of a ridge above the Tywi Valley, are a prominent landmark in these parts, visible from miles around. Close examination of the monument itself reveals an imposing, triangular structure, the slender walls of which enclose nothing but thin air.

Any architectural anti-climax is quickly forgotten, for there is nothing disappointing about the siting of Paxton's Tower. From its perch high above the lush Vale of Tywi a great sweep of scenery comes into view, beginning with the verdant farmlands bordering the snaking Tywi and ending in forested hillsides and high mountains.

🚗 *PAXTON'S TOWER is on a minor road near Llanarthney, a village on the B4300 9 miles east of Carmarthen.*

PEMBREY COUNTRY PARK
Dyfed

Pembrey is an unconventional country park by the sea. First impressions of this 520-acre area of open grassland and pine forest are predictable enough, but at the end of the road a different scene comes into view.

A barrier of sand dunes unexpectedly presents itself, guarding the approach to the Cefn Sidan Sands. Notions of size have to be revised upwards at Cefn Sidan. It curves along Carmarthen Bay further than the eye can see — seven miles in all, making it one of the longest beaches in Wales, and an ideal venue for the sport of land yachting.

Pembrey's unorthodox mixture of coast and countryside encourages all kinds of outdoor activities. The conifer woodlands besides the beach — planted to help stabilise an area which suffers from wind erosion — are popular for nature studies, walking and pony trekking.

🚗 *PEMBREY COUNTRY PARK is accessible off the A484 just west of Burry Port.*

PENCLAWDD AND THE LOUGHOR ESTUARY
West Glamorgan

The north Gower coastline is totally unlike that of the rocky, cliff-backed south. In the emptier north, the low-tide sands, salt flats and marsh beds of the Loughor estuary possess a strange and silent beauty.

Few visitors find their way to spectacularly sited Weobley Castle. This old fortified manor house stands on a grassy hillside overlooking Llanrhidian Marsh, a deep-brown expanse of wetlands gripped by a brooding beauty. Fewer still explore the sand dunes and nature reserve at Whiteford Burrows, on the mouth of the estuary.

The sandy wilderness around Penclawdd still yields a living to the traditional cockle pickers, a hardy breed who rely largely on horse-drawn carts and short-handled rakes, the time-honoured tools of the trade.

🚗 *PENCLAWDD, on the B4295, is 8 miles west of Swansea.*

PORT EYNON
West Glamorgan

This little Gower resort, all alone on its sheltered bay bounded by treacherous cliffs, must have been the perfect smugglers' haunt in its time. The pretty beach now attracts a less clandestine clientele, whilst walkers head north-westwards along what is probably the most spectacular coastal path on the Gower Peninsula.

Two interesting diversions beckon near the start of the walk — the strange Culver Hole, a tall, walled-up section of sea-cliff of mysterious origin, and the ruined Salt House, a vulnerably located mansion destroyed, according to legend, during a fierce 18th-century storm.

The walk, six miles long, treads a wary path on top of sheer limestone cliffs all the way to Worm's Head, passing the inaccessible Paviland Cave where the famous 'Red Lady', a prehistoric skeleton, was discovered.

🚗 *PORT EYNON, on the A4118, is 16 miles west of Swansea.*

PORTHCAWL
Mid Glamorgan

Porthcawl, a leading South Wales seaside resort, has two sides to it. Sandy Bay and Trecco Bay, to the east, share the dubious honour of hosting one of Europe's largest caravan parks and a seafront funfair. To the west, beyond the pretty harbour and sturdy breakwater, a quieter, less colourful Porthcawl takes over.

An attractive esplanade leads to a rocky coast bordered by grassy Lock's Common. Further along still are the peaceful sand and rock pools of Rest Bay, culminating in the lonely headland at Sker Point.

The dunes of Merthyr Mawr Warren, two miles away, cover a vast area. A thin strip of woodland near Merthyr Mawr village just manages to keep the sands from swamping the ivy-clad ruin of Candleston Castle.

🚗 *PORTHCAWL, 6 miles southwest of Bridgend, can be reached by the A4106 or A4229 off the A48.*

The Rhigos mountain road, northern gateway to the Rhondda

THE RHONDDA VALLEYS
Mid Glamorgan

In the 19th century, 'King Coal', the 'black diamond', transformed these valleys from a rural backwater to a teeming, tightly-packed — and tightly-knit — series of mining com-

munities. People poured into the Rhondda Fawr ('Big Rhondda') and Fach ('Little Rhondda') Valleys — and coal poured out to fuel the world's Industrial Revolution.

Much has been written about the mining towns — Treorchy, Treherbert and so on — that grew up as layers of long terraces built into the valley sides. *How Green Was My Valley*, the novel by Richard Llewelyn, expresses in its title the typical view, still current, of an area blighted by coalmining. Those deterred by such inaccurate views miss a gauntly beautiful part of Wales.

Mountainsides and open moorlands, untouched by any form of industry, rise abruptly from once-volatile valley floors. Coalmining is no more, and it is not too optimistic to say that the valleys — thanks to far-reaching environmental improvement schemes — are now becoming green again.

THE RHONDDA VALLEYS *can be approached via Pontypridd and the A4058, Bridgend and Hirwaun (A4061) or Aberdare (B4277).*

RHOSILI AND WORM'S HEAD
West Glamorgan

The Gower Peninsula ends on a high note, a climax of windy cliffs, seemingly endless sands and dizzy viewpoints. To Dylan Thomas, Rhosili beach was 'miles of yellow coldness going away into the distance of the sea'. If he had cared to measure it,

Dylan would have found that the beach is well over three miles long, beginning at the foot of the clifftop village only to end at the faraway Burry Holms headland.

Worm's Head, Rhosili's second spectacular natural feature, is a narrow neck of land pointing bravely into the open seas west of the village. Care should be taken by those venturing on to this wind-scoured, exposed headland, tenuously linked to the mainland by a flooded causeway which is only dry for two-and-a-half hours at low tide.

Petty Officer Edgar Evans, who died on Scott's ill-fated expedition to the Antarctic in 1917, came from this locality. He is remembered by a memorial in Rhosili Church.

RHOSILI, *reached by the B4247 off the A4118, is 18 miles west of Swansea.*

Gower's end — miles of lonely, windswept sand at Rhosili

SWANSEA
West Glamorgan

Dylan Thomas's much-quoted description of this, his birthplace, as an 'ugly, lovely town' contained a convoluted, poetic truth applicable to the Swansea of the early and mid 20th century. Times change; some towns — Swansea, for one — become cities. Dylan, were he resurrected, would hardly recognise his home town of old.

Swansea, Wales's second city, is busy transforming itself into a fresh and airy 'city-by-the-sea' by making the most of its location on a sandy, sheltered bay. Its historic links with the ocean are being re-defined in the new Maritime Quarter, a far-sighted development that includes a 600-berth marina and waterfront village.

A bronze statue of the young Dylan, looking suitably bemused by it all, stands in a brand-new piazza beside the boat-filled marina. Close by are another two recent additions — the Dylan Thomas Theatre and Maritime and Industrial Museum, the latter containing a fully operational woollen mill, rescued from nearby, which produces traditional Welsh weaves.

This go-ahead city, for all its modernity, retains its links with traditional Wales. It is not at all unusual to hear Welsh spoken in the new shopping complexes or the multi-activity (and multi-million pound) leisure centre. Swansea Market is the city's most endearing meeting place of influences old and new. Despite its functional modern appearance, it houses a market place with bags of local character. The market's stallholders sell a tempting array of home cooking and fresh foods, including cockles handpicked from the Penclawdd beds and that unique Welsh dish, laverbread, a black, gooey concoction made from seaweed with a taste that does justice to its unique appearance.

In the city centre, the scant ruins of Swansea Castle, surrounded by office blocks and shops, present an incongruous sight. Amongst the displays of pottery, glass and porcelain in the Glynn Vivian Art Gallery are superb collections of old Swansea and Nantgarw items. In terms of sheer visual extravaganza, nothing can match the Brangwyn Panels in Swansea's Guildhall, a series of huge, warm-toned murals painted by Sir Frank Brangwyn and originally intended for the House of Lords.

SWANSEA is accessible off the M4 and A48, 42 miles west of Cardiff.

30 The Penclawdd cockle women continue to set up shop at Swansea's superb fresh foods market. This is *the* place to buy laverbread

Dylan's Wales

Dylan's statue, Swansea, and the tiny shed in which he worked at **Laugharne**

Wales's brilliant national poet, Dylan Marlais Thomas was born at 5 Cwmdonkin Drive, Swansea, on 27 October 1914. He died, aged only 39, in New York on 9 November 1953. During his all too brief life, Dylan's fame — or notoriety — was probably a product more of his image as a boozy Welsh Bohemian than his seductive literary skills.

As stories of his undoubtedly undisciplined and chaotic private life fade, we are left with what really counts — a solid body of work which places him amongst the great writers of the 20th century. Dylan's inspiration sprang from the people and places, landscapes and locations of South and West Wales. His observations, sometimes through the puzzled, innocent eyes of a child, at others through a filter of weary nostalgia, are mostly evocative, always unique.

Young Dylan cut his teeth on the local newspaper at Swansea. The quality of his early poems served as a passport to greater things, and the precocious boy-poet was soon a familiar figure amongst the London literati. Yet no matter how far he strayed, a nagging umbilical ache always drew him back to South Wales.

Some of the happiest years of his life were spent at sleepy Laugharne. He arrived in May 1949, 'got off the bus, and forgot to get on again'. Here, his poetic genius once again flourished, and he began writing *Under Milk Wood*, arguably his greatest work.

The meticulous love of language he brought to his poetry, and the sense of belonging embodied in his short stories are both combined in *Under Milk Wood*. Set in the imaginary sea-town of Llareggub, this 'play for voices' is a lyrical evocation of everything unique about a small Welsh community not a million miles removed from his beloved Laugharne.

Dylan completed the play just one month before his death. His body was brought back from New York and buried in the churchyard at Laugharne. The Boathouse, where Dylan lived, has been converted into a museum dedicated to his memory. No one, though, has thought to improve on the simple white cross, almost lost amongst a forest of grey tombstones, that marks the poet's final resting place.

Never the pious Welshman, Dylan would not have minded. As well as having a certain way with words, he also possessed a sense of humour. Anyone who has spelt Llareggub backwards will know that.

TINKINSWOOD AND ST LYTHANS BURIAL CHAMBERS
South Glamorgan

This pair of sturdy and striking prehistoric sites stand no more than a mile apart in the farmlands of the Vale of Glamorgan. Tinkinswood is by far the grander of the two. Apart from the absence of a great earthen mound which would have originally covered it, this burial chamber gives the impression of being almost complete.

The chamber's low stone walls, robust and solid, support an enormous slab of rock — the 24 ft-long, 40-ton capstone — across the roof. When Tinkinswood was excavated in 1914, the bones of at least 50 individuals and items of pottery were unearthed.

Tinkinswood is a megalithic monument dating from around 2500 B.C. St Lythans is of the same period though both taller and smaller than its neighbour — tall enough, in fact, to enter without crouching.

BOTH MONUMENTS are off minor roads about 1 mile south of St Nicholas, a village on the A48 6 miles west of Cardiff.

VALE OF NEATH
West Glamorgan

The A465 'Heads of the Valleys' road skirts the high ground above most of the South Wales valleys before swooping down into the Vale of Neath. The efforts made here to recapture the beauty of the valley whilst preserving its rich industrial heritage are beginning to bear fruit.

At the Aberdulais Falls (see separate entry) the National Trust is involved in a major restoration project. The Aberdulais Basin, nearby, is the meeting place of the Neath and Tennant Canals, 19th-century water-ways used to transport coal, iron and many other goods. Parts of the canal have now been rescued from dereliction — especially around the canal basin itself, where there are pleasant towpath walks, picnic sites and an elegant 10-arched aqueduct.

More visitors are also discovering the waterfalls which tumble down through the thickly wooded valley sides. At Pont-Nedd-Fechan, a foot-path leads past an overgrown and long-abandoned silica mine to a series of falls which rank amongst the loveliest in Wales. There are more waterfalls along the opposite side of the valley at Melyncourt, close to picnic sites and woodland walks in the Rheola Forest above Resolven.

Cilfrew, near Aberdulais, is the home of the Penscynor Wildlife Park, a well designed 16-acre parkland site with an international reputation for its world-wide collection of animals and birds. Just west of Neath itself stand the gloomy ruins of Neath Abbey, a 12th-century Cistercian house used, somewhat sacreligiously, for copper and iron smelting during the Industrial Revolution.

NEATH, at the junction of the A465 and A474, is 8 miles east of Swansea.

WELSH FOLK MUSEUM
South Glamorgan

This museum performs a distance-shrinking trick — with elements of time travel thrown in for good measure — by taking visitors on a trip around the rural Wales of old in one afternoon. At least half a day is needed to do justice to the Welsh Folk Museum, the great fascination of which lies out-of-doors amongst the trees in extensive, grassy parklands where old buildings rescued from all over Wales have been lovingly reconstructed stone-by-stone, timber-by-timber.

The buildings — around 20 in all — include a humble farmworker's cottage, large farmhouse, cruck-built barn, woollen factory, tannery, smithy, cockpit, traditional chapel and tiny toll-house which still displays its list of charges. Domestic and cultural life in the Wales of bygone times is also preserved within a modern, purpose-built museum block where imaginatively presented displays highlight everything from furniture to farming methods, costumes to medical care.

The third side to this multi-faceted site is represented by a fine Elizabethan country house, the 100-acre grounds and gardens of which accommodate the entire museum. The mansion, an imposing, many-gabled affair with a typically opulent Long Gallery (a favourite 16th-century feature) and Flemish tapestries, is also open to the public.

🚗 *THE MUSEUM, 4½ miles from the centre of Cardiff, is in the village of St Fagan's on the western outskirts of the city.*

Left: **The Welsh Folk Museum is now the home of this toll-house, which once stood near Aberystwyth**

WELSH MINERS' MUSEUM AND AFAN ARGOED COUNTRY PARK
West Glamorgan

The harsh realities of 'coal getting' are neither sensationalised nor treated sentimentally at this thought-provoking little museum. From the outside, it looks rather plain and ordinary. Within the confines of modest dimensions and budgets it manages to accommodate all manner of exhibits and items, putting many a more affluent museum to shame.

Quite deservedly, this museum has attracted a number of awards for the insight it gives into the life and work of the South Wales miner in the unforgiving 19th century. The 'good old, bad old' days of that tumultuous century, which brought catastrophic changes to this part of Wales, are recalled in all manner of ways. Old newspapers tell of terrible mining disasters; miners' lamps and the tools-of-the-trade are displayed; and visitors are taken into the collier's home through a re-created kitchen scene and transported right to the pit face along a reconstructed underground gallery.

The museum stands on the flanks of a tree-lined hillside at the entrance to the Afan Argoed Country Park in the Afan Valley. This vale, known locally as 'Little Switzerland', is one of the most scenic of the South Wales valleys. Evidence of its coal-mining past is now almost exclusively confined to the museum thanks to large-scale landscaping and conifer planting schemes.

🚗 *THE MUSEUM is on the A4017 near Cymmer, approximately 15 miles east of Swansea.*

Right: **A claustrophobic coal-face in the Welsh Miners' Museum**

West Wales

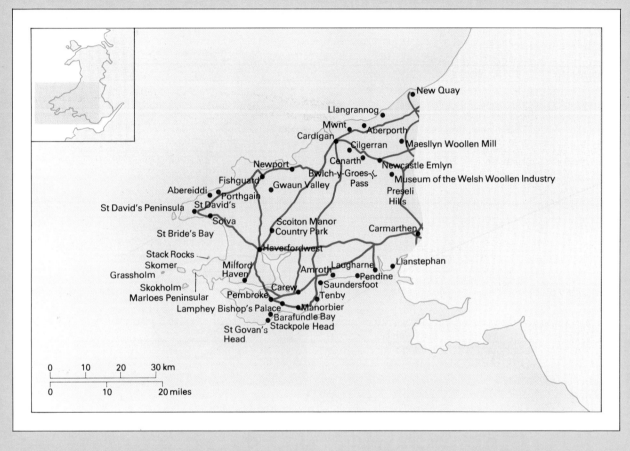

THE SEA HAS ALWAYS been the dominant element here. Iron Age man was drawn to promontory forts overlooking the waves. Celtic saints made perilous journeys across the waters, spreading the Christian message. As the Dark Ages descended, Viking raiders plundered the coast. The Normans, in their turn, built castles such as Pembroke and Kidwelly with sea-borne access.

West Wales's extraordinarily rich coastal heritage — in scenery as well as pure history — manifests itself most strongly within the Pembrokeshire Coast National Park. Pembrokeshire is unique as the only one of Britain's ten national parks which is almost entirely coastal-based. At 225 square miles, it is also Britain's smallest: a misleading statistic. The figure that really counts is its 230 miles of seashore.

The park runs from Poppit Sands near Cardigan to Amroth. Pembrokeshire's tide-washed sea-cliffs and sandy bays have tested the pen of many a writer, provoking this 17th-century description of an area 'shaped with divers corners ...... in some places concave, in some convex, but in most .... bending inwards as doth the Moon'.

West Wales also embraces the southern stretch of Cardigan Bay around New Quay and the silent sands near Laugharne, two areas rich in Dylan Thomas associations. Inland, there are the old market and weaving towns and maze of unexplored, leafy lanes around the Teifi Valley, an enchanting, gentle swathe of countryside.

ABERPORTH
Dyfed

Aberporth's twin beaches — each one a neat crescent of sands — today play host to summer visitors. In the 18th and 19th centuries, they provided safe and sheltered anchorage for the coastal traders of Cardigan Bay and the largest fleet of herring boats in Wales.

The old boats, long since departed, have not given way to garish seaside developments. Aberporth, although busy in summer, is largely uncommercialised, retaining the atmosphere of a village-by-the-sea. Its houses fit themselves in as best they can amongst towering cliff scenery, a dominant feature along this stretch of Cardigan Bay. East of Aberporth, a path leads across the blustery headlands for just over a mile to tiny Tresaith, where a waterfall plunges onto sea-rocks next to a small, cliff-backed beach. Beyond Tresaith lies Traeth Penbryn, one of the loveliest stretches of sand on Cardigan Bay.

ABERPORTH, accessible by the B4333 off the A487, is 6 miles north-east of Cardigan.

CARDIGAN
Dyfed

This handsome old town is a meeting place for country and coast, the River Teifi and the sea. Cardigan has led a varied life as a Norman stronghold, sea-port, market town and farming centre.

Each of these different periods is etched on the face of the town. The ruined battlements and round towers of a castle put up in early medieval times to control the river mouth stand on a rise above Cardigan's most picturesque feature, an elegant, five-arched bridge, 17th century in origin.

On the opposite bank, tall wharfside warehouses, now mostly converted, are reminders of Cardigan's role as a busy trading port. The charming covered market, beneath the equally attractive Guildhall, is still going strong, providing for the farming communities from around and about.

Today, this mix of market and sea-town has an added dimension, for Cardigan is now a well-situated holiday centre for those wishing to explore the coves and headlands of both Cardigan Bay and the Pembrokeshire Coast National Park. The national park starts on a high note at nearby St Dogmael's, taking in the sandy Teifi estuary and craggy Cemaes Head.

St Dogmael's itself grew up around its Benedictine abbey, founded in 1115, the remains of which are still visible. At the Cardigan Wildlife Park, a few miles south of the town, many types of animal, including exotic breeds, can be seen at close quarters.

Cardigan enjoys a special status in traditional Welsh circles, for Wales's first eisteddfod (see special feature, page 109) was reputedly held here in 1176.

CARDIGAN is accessible by the A487 from Fishguard, A478 from Tenby and A484 from Carmarthen.

CAREW
Dyfed

Man's early religious preoccupations, his medieval military and social ambitions and more recent exploitation of the mechanical age all put in an appearance at this pretty hamlet, on the upper reaches of the tidal Carew River.

A roadside Celtic cross, slender, tall and heavily decorated with interlacing patterns, bears an inscription which commemorates

Carew, one of Wales's more comfortable, domesticated castles

Maredudd ap Edwin, King of Dyfed, who was killed in battle in 1035. Regarded as one of the finest 11th-century crosses in Britain, it has been adopted as the official symbol of Cadw, the newly created government body responsible for many of Wales's historic monuments.

A splendid castle stands on the grassy riverbanks across the field. Carew Castle, originally a medieval stronghold built here to take advantage of seaborne access via the waters of the Milford Haven, gradually evolved into a handsome Tudor and Elizabethan home. Its purely decorative mullioned windows are a particular visual treat.

Carew Tidal Mill is unique in Wales. As its name implies, this 19th-century mill — which replaced an earlier model — takes advantage of the rise and fall in the river. It stands, three storeys tall, on a dam which traps the high-tide waters, subsequently released to power the waterwheel.

CAREW, near the junction of the A4075 and A477, is 4 miles north-east of Pembroke.

Photographers have been coming to Teifiside's Cenarth Falls since the early days of the camera

CARMARTHEN
Dyfed

The 'capital' of the old county of Carmarthenshire is now the main administrative centre for the huge new 'super-county' of Dyfed, created by local government reorganisation in 1974. The imposing county offices stand on a hill above the River Tywi, sharing a site with the remains of Carmarthen's medieval castle.

Fragments of castle wall and ruined towers appear unexpectedly amongst more modern architecture. The town itself is a pleasant mixture of old and new. Narrow lanes, clearly medieval in origin, lead into wide shopping streets and pedestrianised areas where white-collar office workers mingle with ruddy-faced farming folk.

The best time to visit Carmarthen is on a Wednesday, when the market is in full swing. The animal pens and auction yards behind the covered market are a buzz of activity, as farmers from many miles around haggle over the best prices for their cattle and sheep.

The Romans ventured no further west than Carmarthen. They constructed an amphitheatre here, one of only seven known in Britain, its shape still clearly imprinted in a grassy hollow on the eastern outskirts of town.

Carmarthen Museum, at nearby Abergwili, is based within a lovely old range of buildings, the former Palace of the Bishop of St David's, dating from 1283. Its most talked-about exhibit, a wizened tree stump, recalls Carmarthen's legendary Arthurian connections. This is the famous Merlin's Oak, rescued from its original site during redevelopment presumably to protect the town from the prophecy: 'When Merlin's Oak shall tumble down, then shall fall Carmarthen town.'

CARMARTHEN is on the junction of the A40, A48 and A484, approximately 27 miles north-west of Swansea.

CENARTH
Dyfed

No Victorian Grand Tour of Wales was complete without a visit to the falls at Cenarth. Here, the River Teifi's normally sedate progress is interrupted as it tumbles over rocks before rushing beneath a picturesque old stone bridge.

The Teifi is a river famed for its salmon and sewin (the Welsh name for sea-trout) fishing. It has long been associated with the coracle, a tiny fishing craft made of intertwined laths of hazel and willow, which has been used in Wales for at least 2000 years. These bobbing, precarious looking one-man boats, which resemble an upturned umbrella, are extremely manoeuvrable in skilled hands. They can still sometimes be seen at Cenarth — for a guaranteed siting, come during the coracle races held each August.

The riverbanks here, a repository of fishing lore and traditions, are an appropriate setting for the Cenarth Fishing Museum, where angling enthusiasts can ponder over a huge collection of rods and reels.

CENARTH is on the A484 between Cardigan and Newcastle Emlyn.

CILGERRAN
Dyfed

A Victorian writer, stalking the remains of Cilgerran Castle 'beautiful in its ruins', was overcome by an attack of purple prose, an occupational hazard at that time. His imagination — and pen — ran riot when he wrote: 'Looking from the lofty ruin on the embowered glen below one wonders how the passions of war could rage amid such loveliness. But Teifi's silver flood has been crimsoned with human blood.'

A little over the top, perhaps, but excusable, for Cilgerran sets off the romantically minded. Legend surrounds this Norman stronghold from which, reputedly, Nest, the beautiful wife of Gerald of Wales, was kidnapped by a Welsh prince in 1109. On a sounder historic note, the castle led an active life in the 12th and 13th centuries, when it was captured and recaptured a number of times.

Today, its great attraction lies in its location. Cilgerran's walls and towers, though powerful enough, cannot compete with its setting on a sheer crag above a deep and lushly wooded gorge carved by the River Teifi. When the Victorians came here on their Grand Tour of Wales, coracles (see Cenarth entry for further details) would have been a common sight on these waters. Today, they are mainly confined to a coracle regatta, held every August.

CILGERRAN, on a minor road off the A478, is 3 miles south-east of Cardigan.

DALE PENINSULA
Dyfed

This peninsula is one of the windiest places in Britain, where gusts have been known to exceed 100 m.p.h. In compensation, it is also one of the sunniest, with an annual average of 1800 hours of sunshine.

Dale is a place of extremes. This 'place apart' sits right at the end of the road in a far corner of Pembrokeshire, steadfastly ignoring the comings and goings of the outside world. Although no more than three miles from tip to toe, its largely remote coastline — Dale is the definitive place for walkers and naturalists — is one of the most wildly beautiful in Wales.

Extremes in contrast are also part of Dale's character. Its west-facing cliffs bear the full force of the winds whilst the bays along the east coast look inwards to the calm and sheltered waters of the Milford Haven. The Vikings, when they plundered Wales in the Dark Ages, must have used this sheltered anchorage, for *Dale*, meaning 'valley', is a pure Norse name.

The coastguard and lighthouse station at St Anne's Head, at the entrance to the Haven, keeps a watchful eye on the giant supertankers that glide in and out of this busy waterway. In 1485, a much frailer flotilla landed at nearby Mill Bay, bearing Welshman Harri Tudur and his supporters. From here, Harri marched to victory over Richard III at the Battle of Bosworth, becoming Henry VII, first of the Tudors, initiator of a mighty dynasty.

🚗 *DALE is on the B4327, 12 miles south-west of Haverfordwest.*

FISHGUARD
Dyfed

This is a town of many parts. Goodwick is a commercial port, the end of the line for the Paddington to Fishguard rail link and the embarkation point for the Irish Sea ferries. The town centre and main shopping streets are to be found on the hill, in Upper Fishguard. Call in at the Town Hall, not only for its excellent little covered market but also to see the mementos of Fishguard's seafaring past — including a record of ships rescued by the local lifeboat.

Lower Fishguard, an inlet protected by steep, gorse-covered hillsides, is by far the prettiest part of town. The old harbourside here, lined with its row of gabled cottages, paints the perfect picture of a self-contained and timeless quayside community. Full advantage was taken of the location when it became Llareggub, Dylan Thomas's imaginary, magical sea-town, during the filming of *Under Milk Wood* which starred Elizabeth Taylor and the late Richard Burton.

Carreg Wastad Point, a remote headland north of the town, appears in the record books as the scene, in 1797, of the last invasion of Britain. French troops, led by an American colonel, initiated this farcical, half-cocked affair, which ended in ignominious surrender almost before it had begun. An interesting range of invasion memorabilia can be seen in the Royal Oak Inn, opposite the Town Hall.

🚗 *FISHGUARD, on the junction of the A487 and A40, is half-way between Cardigan and St Davids.*

The Graham Sutherland Art Gallery, within Picton Castle

GWAUN VALLEY
Dyfed

Residents of this sheltered, secluded valley deep in the backwoods of north Pembrokeshire are, quite literally, a little behind the times — during the New Year, at least. When Britain adopted changes to the calendar in 1752 which threw everything forward by 11 days, news cannot have filtered through to the Gwaun Valley; either that, or its diehard residents chose to ignore it. As a consequence, its inhabitants still celebrate New Year's Day on 13 January. During the day, folk from the scattered farms and cottages get together for a meal of goose and plum pudding accompanied by traditional celebrations whilst the children collect *calennig*, a New Year's gift of money, apples and oranges.

The valley's ancient, hanging woodlands lend this hideaway a secretive, untouched air. Oakwoods in the main, they clothe steep valley sides above the Gwaun, its waters rushing by on their way to Lower Fishguard and the sea.

THE GWAUN VALLEY, a few miles south-east of Fishguard, is accessible by minor road off the B4313.

HAVERFORDWEST
Dyfed

Before boundary changes in 1974, this was Pembrokeshire's county town. Although the old county, officially at least, no longer exists, Haverfordwest clings to its status as 'capital' of this part of the world. The Pembrokeshire Coast National Park headquarters are located here, together with many administrative and local government offices. Moreover, Haverfordwest's historic pedigree is impeccable.

Haverfordwest has all the characteristics of a river town. It grew up around a hilltop Norman castle which guarded the highest navigable point on the Western Cleddau, a river leading into the mighty Milford Haven waterway. A maze of narrow, steep streets, lined with grand Georgian buildings, points not only to the town's great age but also to its past prosperity as a port. Its trading links with the West of England are perpetuated most strongly in the name of the Bristol Trader Inn which stands in Quay Street next to old warehouses where wool and wine were stored.

Further along the quay, an attractive new riverside shopping complex blends in well with its historic surroundings. The shell of Haverfordwest Castle gazes over the rooftops of an architecturally fascinating town which also contains three interesting churches (St Mary's is particularly lovely). An old gaol, built into the castle, is now the home of the County Museum.

Haverfordwest's central location, roughly equidistant from the coastlines of south, west and north Pembrokeshire (the name lives on despite the politicians) makes it a popular touring centre. The grounds of Picton Castle, a few miles to the south-east, contain the Graham Sutherland Art Gallery, the largest permanent display anywhere in the world of works by this distinguished artist, who found much of his inspiration in Pembrokeshire.

HAVERFORDWEST, on the junction of the A40, A4076 and A487, is 15 miles from Fishguard and 10 miles from Pembroke.

Lamphey Bishop's Palace, used as a country retreat by the medieval churchmen of St David's

LAMPHEY BISHOP'S PALACE
Dyfed

The prelates of the medieval church were no strangers to creature comforts. At Lamphey, the bishops of St David's had a comfortable retreat where they could lead the lives of country gentlemen amongst pleasant surroundings which contained orchards, vegetable gardens and a fishpond.

The former splendour of this large ruin, partly hidden behind low walls, has not entirely vanished. A large grassy enclosure leads to a group of buildings in the far corner of the grounds, decorated with arcaded parapets — an architectural embellishment reminiscent, not surprisingly, of the Bishop's Palace in St David's itself.

The shell of the Great Hall is most impressive, as is the attractive 16th-century chapel, noted for its five-light east window. The gatehouse is a strange sight. Nowadays, this castellated little tower, a mixture of ecclesiastic and military architectural influences, stands isolated in the middle of the enclosure, guarding nothing but grass.

THE PALACE is in the village of Lamphey, on the A4139 2 miles east of Pembroke.

LAUGHARNE
Dyfed

Sleepy Laugharne is indelibly linked with the life and work of poet and writer Dylan Marlais Thomas (see special feature, page **31**). Dylan discovered Laugharne in the 1940s, spending one of the happiest and most productive periods of his life here beside its 'heron-priested shore'.

He lived in the Georgian Boathouse, within sight and sound of the seabirds and lapping waves of the sandy Taf estuary. Laugharne continues to fit Dylan's soothing description of it as a 'timeless, mild, beguiling island of a town'. Increasing numbers of visitors now follow in Dylan's footsteps.

They walk along the narrow cliff path to the Boathouse, which has been converted into a museum dedicated to his life and work, passing on the approach to the house a small hut — no more than a glorified garden shed really — in which he would lock himself away to write. Laugharne appeared everywhere in his work, finally blending with his memories of another sea-town, New Quay, to become imaginary, magical Llareggub in *Under Milk Wood*.

Laugharne Castle ('as brown as owls' according to Dylan) is a sprawling mysterious ruin, part medieval fortification, part Tudor palace. Its romantic, ivy-covered walls and towers (currently under restoration) caught the eye of artist J.M.W. Turner over 250 years ago, when he captured it on canvas.

🚗 *LAUGHARNE is on the A4066, 13 miles south-west of Carmarthen.*

The little resort of Llangrannog shelters beneath some of Cardigan Bay's finest cliff scenery

LLANGRANNOG
Dyfed

A narrow glen winds its way through wooded countryside to open up to the sea at Llangrannog. This picturesque little village of colourfully painted cottages and houses has grown up around a sandy beach on one of the few breaks in the headlands.

Steep steps, cut into the cliff above the beach, mark the start of one of the most spectacular coast paths on Cardigan Bay. The path skirts a hillside crowned by an Iron Age fort before leading to the promontory of Ynys Lochtyn, one mile north-east of Llangrannog. The cliff-backed shoreline suddenly seems tame in comparison to this exposed, sea-washed and wind-scoured promontory, a thin finger of land — its tip often cut off by the waves — pointing into Cardigan Bay.

Appearances at Ynys Lochtyn are not deceptive — caution should be exercised here, and when the winds are high it is best viewed from a secure distance.

🚗 *LLANGRANNOG is on the B4334, accessible off the A487, about 13 miles north-east of Cardigan.*

LLANSTEPHAN
Dyfed

This neat little community, a one-time fishing village, clusters around its church on the sandy banks of the Tywi estuary. The church's 13th-century tower, though sturdy and battlemented, is thoroughly eclipsed by the ruins of Llanstephan Castle, a grey and brooding pile on the bluff above the brightly painted village.

The castle's coarse stone walls and towers spread themselves across a strategic site exploited by man since prehistoric times. Items from the 6th century B.C. have been found here on

Iron Age man and medieval warlord sought security at Llanstephan

the site of an Iron Age promontory fort. When the Normans arrived, they cleared out the prehistoric ditches, incorporating parts of the ancient fort into their plan. The castle gradually grew up over the next few hundred years. Its twin-towered Great Gatehouse, by far its most imposing feature, enjoys expansive views across the mouth of the estuary to Worm's Head on the tip of the Gower Peninsula.

LLANSTEPHAN is on the B4312, 8 miles south-west of Carmarthen.

MAESLLYN WOOLLEN MILL AND MUSEUM OF THE WELSH WOOLLEN INDUSTRY
Dyfed

Until early this century, the banks of the River Teifi and its tributaries around Llandysul echoed to the clatter of many a woollen mill. 'Hardly a spot (remained) on any stream where it would be convenient to build another mill,' so it was said. Some survive, others have been revived, perpetuating a tradition of woollen weaving that stretches back many centuries in Wales (see special feature, page 58).

Maesllyn's revival came in 1976. Disused and derelict, it has been renovated as a working mill-cum-museum. Early hand-operated looms and 19th-century mechanical weaving frames illustrate the evolution in production methods. Displays also explain the entire production process, from raw wool to finished cloth.

Across the Teifi, a few miles to the south, is the Museum of the Welsh Woollen Industry, part of the National Museum of Wales. Here, old photographs, a 'Factory Trail' and an extensive collection of textile machinery and hand tools tell the story of Wales's most important rural industry from the Middle Ages to the present day.

MAESLLYN is located on a minor road, most easily accessible off the A486 at Croes-lan crossroads 4 miles north-west of Llandysul. The Museum of the Welsh Woollen Industry is at Drefach Felindre, 3 miles south-east of Newcastle Emlyn, by minor road off the A484.

MANORBIER
Dyfed

This select little village-cum-resort boasts the definitive castle-by-the-sea. Manorbier Castle stands on a bluff above the bay, with unbroken views across the sands and surf.

Built by the Norman de Barri family in the 12th and 13th centuries, this fortress is in an excellent state of repair, its baronial character undiminished by the years. The castle was the birthplace, in 1146, of Giraldus Cambrensis, Gerald of Wales, a monk and chronicler to whom we owe much of our knowledge of life in medieval Wales. Both native Welsh and Norman newcomers are subjected to his authoritative and impartial gaze in two classic works, *Itinerary* and *Description*, based on his travels throughout Wales.

Giraldus's objectivity possibly wavered when it came to writing about his birthplace, which he described as 'the pleasantest spot in Wales', though it is often endorsed by those who find Manorbier a more peaceful alternative to busier Tenby.

MANORBIER is on the B4585 (off the A4139) 5 miles south-west of Tenby.

MARLOES PENINSULA
Dyfed

Few people make the long trek west to Marloes; which is good news for those who do, for they have one of Pembrokeshire's finest beaches all to themselves. Marloes Sands, a half-mile walk from the car park, is totally uncommercialised, uninhabited and undeveloped, a rare combination of characteristics even in Pembrokeshire. The beach, a gentle curve of firm sands backed by a low line of rosy-red cliffs, ends at Gateholm Island, accessible at low tide, on which the native Welsh lived during Roman times.

Marloes itself, although landlocked, was once a fishing village. Its harbour was at Martin's Haven, two miles to the west. This tiny inlet, equipped with nothing more than a slipway and winch, is now the embarkation point for summer boat trips to Skomer Island (see separate entry). Martin's Haven is close to the Deer Park headland, a starkly beautiful promontory with exceptional cliff scenery, once inhabited by Iron Age man.

MARLOES is accessible off the B4327, 12 miles south-west of Haverfordwest.

MILFORD HAVEN WATERWAY
Dyfed

The boundary of the Pembrokeshire Coast National Park takes a short detour along the Milford Haven to avoid the oil terminals and petrochemical installations stationed midway along this magnificent deepwater inlet. Admiral Lord Nelson regarded this waterway as one of the finest sheltered harbours in the world. Deserted block-house fortifications, constructed along the Haven in the 19th century to dissuade the French from any thought of attack, are ghostly guardians of the large naval dockyards which were once located here.

The Haven, also busy with deepsea fishing fleets in the past, continues to keep itself occupied. Judged on tonnage handled, it is Britain's second largest port, a position achieved thanks to the massive oil cargoes transported by the giant supertankers that berth here, beside jetties linked to a steely web of oil storage and processing plants.

The new road bridge north of Pembroke spans a great divide in the Haven. Beyond this point, the national park once again reasserts itself along the Daugleddau, a peaceful backwater of tidal creeks and wooded shores.

🚗 THE MILFORD HAVEN — upstream and downstream — can be explored by boat trips from Hobb's Point, Pembroke Dock, 2 miles north-west of Pembroke.

MWNT
Dyfed

Everything is in miniature at tiny Mwnt, tucked away on a secluded stretch of Cardigan Bay coastline. Miniature beach, mountain and church are the ingredients of this delightful spot, now in the care of the National Trust.

Mwnt simply means 'mound', a prosaic reference to the headland and viewpoint which towers above the beach. More deservedly, this perfectly formed crescent of sand has also been labelled 'the jewel of Cardigan Bay'.

The Church of the Holy Cross shares the grassy hillside between beach and headland with munching sheep. Whitewashed, austere, solid and very old indeed, with an ancient wood-beamed roof, it has stood here since medieval times, possibly on the site of a religious settlement founded during the 'Age of Saints' in the 5th and 6th centuries.

For all its beauty, Mwnt has its darker side. Up until a few centuries ago, games were held here on the first Sunday in January called Sul Coch y Mwnt ('The Bloody Sunday of the Mound') to commemorate the violent defeat of a Flemish landing on the coast here in 1155.

🚗 MWNT, on the coast between the Teifi estuary and Aberporth, is accessible by minor road about 5 miles north-east of Cardigan.

PEMBROKE
Dyfed

This Norman outpost quickly graduated from its original crude stake and timber stronghold to a mighty fortress, one of the finest in Wales. Pembroke Castle is no tumbledown ruin. It struts, purposeful and well preserved, on a rock above the town and river, its strategic importance and stature plain to see.

The castle is a legacy mostly from the late 12th century and the ambitions of nobleman William Marshall. Later — in 1457 — it was the birthplace of Harri Tudur, the Welshman who became Henry VII, initiator of the mighty Tudor dynasty.

Only from within the walls does the castle reveal its full size and most outstanding feature — the circular Great Keep. For the best view of fortress, river and town, climb to the top of the keep, up a staircase cut into its 20-ft thick walls. From here, the Victorian assessment of Pembroke (akin to 'the skeleton of an ill-conditioned flounder, the castle precinct being the head ...... the only street representing the vertebral bone ......') can be tested for accuracy.

Unflattering though it may sound, the simile does put things into perspective. The town itself occupies a defensive site, its long main street following a narrow spine of high ground which leads away from the castle. But the assessment does not take into account Pembroke's graceful Georgian buildings, nor the pleasant riverside promenade and intact stretches of 14th-century town walls, rare in Britain today.

The hill opposite the castle is occupied by the bulky, and very old, Church of St Nicholas, once part of a medieval Benedictine priory. Pembroke's National Museum of Gypsy Caravans lives up to its rather grand title by containing a marvellous collection of highly decorated, horse-drawn homes, each one a mobile work of art.

🚗 PEMBROKE, at the junction of the A477 and A4139, is 13 miles west of Tenby.

Within these walls was born Harri Tudur, the Welshman better known as Henry VII, first of the Tudor monarchs. Pembroke Castle made its last historic mark when it was besieged by Oliver Cromwell for seven weeks

NEWCASTLE EMLYN
Dyfed

Livestock marts are held at Newcastle Emlyn every Friday. This old market town, located smack in the midst of the loveliest stretch of the Teifi Valley, has faithfully served the farming communities scattered throughout Teifiside's 'low hills and wooded vales' for many centuries.

Its ruined castle, although intended more as a country seat than military stronghold, makes the most of the protection afforded by a naturally fortified loop in the river. A mile downstream, the Teifi is joined by a tributary, the Ceri. This little river, flowing through a secluded, small and perfectly silent valley just north of Newcastle Emlyn, powers the waterwheel of the Felin Geri Flourmill. Dating from the 17th century, this mill was saved from dereliction in the 1970s and is now open to the public. Its creaking wheels, wooden cogs and grinders are operational once more, producing stoneground wholemeal flour exactly as it was milled 100 years ago.

🚗 *NEWCASTLE EMLYN, at the Junction of the A484 and A475, is 11 miles south-east of Cardigan.*

NEWPORT
Dyfed

Newport typifies the smallish resorts which are strung out irregularly along the rugged north Pembrokeshire coastline. The beach, on the shores of Newport Bay where the River Nevern meets the sea, is a little way from the old town.

Competing with the sands for the visitor's attention are a wealth of historic sites, scattered around the district. The moody Pentre Ifan Cromlech (see Preseli Hills entry) stands nearby. Mynydd Carningli, a 1000-ft outcrop in the Preseli Hills above the town, is littered with remains of a sturdy Iron Age hill-fort. Newport itself, a medieval charter town which still hangs on to its time-honoured ceremonial customs, is full of interest. A group of prehistoric burial chambers can be seen beside the main road, just over one mile west of Newport. And at Cwm yr Eglwys, at the foot of Dinas Head, there are the seashore remains of a church destroyed by a great gale in 1859.

🚗 *NEWPORT is on the A487 between Fishguard and Cardigan.*

NEW QUAY
Dyfed

The quayside here preserves so effectively the look of the last century that it seems as if the old list of 'tolls and dues', displayed on the harbour wall, might still apply. The list is a leftover from the times when the waters of Cardigan Bay were busy with trading vessels.

At New Quay, we learn that they paid three pence to unload soap, six pence for ham, one shilling for bath chairs and two shillings for coffins.

The harbour, completely protected from the westerly winds by New Quay Head, is one of the most sheltered along Cardigan Bay. Crab and lobster boats still work from here, and it is not too difficult — apart from during those peak times in summer when the narrow, steep streets are busy with visitors — to evoke parallels with Llareggub, the imaginary sea-town in *Under Milk Wood*, which Dylan Thomas based on times spent here and at his home at Laugharne.

🚗 *NEW QUAY, accessible by the A486 and B4342 off the A487, is between Cardigan and Aberystwyth.*

Enclosed in a fold of green hills, Cwm Tudu beach at New Quay

PENDINE
Dyfed

A flat, wide corridor of sands stretches into the far distance from the rocky headland above Pendine village to Ginst Point near Laugharne. This served as a battleground for the world land speed record attempts in the 1920s. The two protagonists, Sir Malcolm Campbell in *Bluebird* and Welsh ace J.G. Parry Thomas in *Babs*, sped down this five-mile long beach until, in 1927, the inevitable happened. When attempting to recapture the title by beating Campbell's record-breaking 174.88 m.p.h., Parry Thomas lost control. *Babs* careered into a series of sickening cartwheels, killing its driver. The wreck was buried in the dunes but has since been exhumed.

Pendine Sands can catch out even the most staid and slow driver. A notice at the entrance ramp to the beach says it all: 'Danger. Do not drive or park near the water's edge. On average, ten cars a year are submerged by the sea.' You have been warned.

🚗 *PENDINE is at the junction of the A4066 and B4314, 18 miles south-west of Carmarthen.*

PORTHGAIN AND ABEREIDDI
Dyfed

Porthgain is a great polariser of opinions. Some find the intrusion of 19th-century brickworks into this otherwise idyllic harbourside downright ugly. Others are captivated by the strange beauty of this nautical and industrial site.

No more than a handful of houses and harbour pub — the Sloop Inn, founded, according to the date above the door, in 1743 — Porthgain remained undisturbed as a tiny haven for centuries. Transformation took

place in the mid 19th century. Slate and granite, quarried from the headlands, were exported from here to the burgeoning industrial towns hungry for building materials, and a brickworks grew up along the harbourside.

By the 1930s, it was all over. The abandoned ruins now stand incongruously amongst some of the most silent and serrated coastal scenery in Wales. Across the headland, at Abereiddi, there are more remnants of industrial activity. Beyond the 'black-sand' beach (formed by the action of the waves on the slate and shale cliffs) and ruined workers' cottages is the eerie 'blue lagoon', an abandoned slate quarry flooded by the sea.

Porthgain harbour is a neat little place, transformed in the mid 19th century by the addition of a brickworks

🚗 *PORTHGAIN and Abereiddi are on minor roads off the A487, approximately 6 miles north-east of St David's.*

PRESELI HILLS
Dyfed

The boundary of the Pembrokeshire Coast National Park faithfully hugs the shoreline for the vast majority of its length, venturing inland just once to embrace the smooth, bare flanks of these hills. The Preselis rise to a high point of 1760 ft at Foel Cwm-cerwyn, their rough pastures and moorland presenting a strange contrast to the rocks and headlands of the nearby shoreline.

These hills are a treasure chest for those interested in prehistory. Prehistoric man's preference for high places has left a rich legacy of ancient monuments, hill-forts and standing stones (see Newport, Dyfed entry). The most famous of all is the Pentre Ifan Cromlech, in the northern foothills a few miles south-east of Newport. This striking burial chamber never fails to provoke mystery and speculation. Its huge 16 ft capstone and three upright supports are made from the same Preseli 'blue stone' that found its way — somehow — to Stonehenge on Salisbury Plain, almost 200 miles away.

THE PRESELI HILLS lie within a southern arc between Cardigan and Fishguard.

ST BRIDE'S BAY
Dyfed

The Pembrokeshire coast is a battleground defined by the wildly varying fortunes of sea and land. The waves are winning conclusively along St Bride's Bay, where the pounding surf bites deeply into soft rocks. To the north and south, the tougher underlying rocks of the St David's and Marloes Peninsulas are able to make an effective stand against the tempestuous sea.

South of Solva, cliffs give way to a long, unbroken stretch of sands at Newgale, a west-facing beach popular with surfers and swimmers. Further south still, a succession of 'Havens' — Nolton, Madoc's, Druidston, Broad and Little — dot the shore. Of these, the small resorts of Broad and Little Haven, with their modest selection of holiday accommodation, are the most popular and easily reached.

NEWGALE is on the A487. Broad and Little Haven are accessible by the B4341 from Haverfordwest.

ST DAVID'S
Dyfed

Britain's smallest city stands isolated on its gale-tossed peninsula in the far-flung south-western corner of Wales. The building responsible for St David's city status — its cathedral — is not immediately visible. It squats, low and discreet, in a grassy hollow well below the rooftops.

The full magnitude of this large, cruciform cathedral is only apparent from the top of the Thirty-nine Steps which lead down to a site that has witnessed Christian worship for 1500 years. *Dewi Sant*, St David, Wales's patron saint, founded a monastic community here in the 6th century which became a fountainhead for the Christian message during Britain's Dark Ages.

Welsh leeks and daffodils make a mass appearance every 1 March, St David's Day, to commemorate this Celtic saint's death in A.D. 589. His city has been an important Christian shrine since medieval times when it was declared that two pilgrimages to St David's would equal one to Rome.

The cathedral, built of a purple-hued local stone and dating from 1176 remains in essence a supreme example of medieval religious architecture, though it has inevitably been much restored over the centuries. Its treasures — far too many to list — include an ornately carved 15th-century oak roof and original late-Norman nave.

The shell of the 14th-century Bishop's Palace, in the field opposite, now has the look of a poor relation. In its time, it would have been a grand and desirable residence which proclaimed the worldly wealth of the medieval church. Although in ruin, traces of its original opulence remain, especially in its fine arcades and elaborate windows.

ST DAVID'S is on the A487, 16 miles north-west of Haverfordwest.

ST DAVID'S PENINSULA
Dyfed

This atmospheric and unpopulated peninsula, formed of tough, sea-resistant rocks, is dotted with religious and historic sites. Whitesands Bay, the only large beach along its rock-strewn coastline, lies beneath a 600-ft high headland which bears evidence of prehistoric and Iron Age settlement.

At St Justinian's, a lifeboat station just manages to squeeze itself in amongst the cliffs overlooking the dangerous waters which separate Ramsey Island from the mainland. Non, mother of St David, is

remembered a little further along the coast at the ruined St Non's Chapel and Holy Well, on green slopes overlooking St Non's Bay. The sheltered creek at Porth Clais, west of St Non's Bay, was once the port for St David's when men and goods always travelled by sea instead of by road.

Caerfai and Caerbwdi, further east, are a pair of little bays separated by yet another rugged headland.

🚗 ALL THE SITES mentioned are no more than a few miles from St David's. Most are accessible by car. All can be explored by following the relevant section of the long-distance Pembrokeshire Coast Footpath.

SAUNDERSFOOT AND AMROTH
Dyfed

Both places are located along the western arc of Carmarthen Bay on a coastline which alternates between rock, shingle and sand. Saundersfoot, by far the larger of the two, has grown up around its commodious harbour, invariably filled with a bobbing, colourful flotilla of holiday boats. Those who know Saundersfoot only as the premier yachting centre in South Wales are amazed to discover that this pretty resort, with its long, sheltered beach, was once a coal-exporting port.

The Pembrokeshire Coast National Park runs as far as Amroth, a few miles to the north-east of Saundersfoot. This coastal hamlet strings itself out along a thin strip of land between wooded slopes and the sea. From its tall beach-front bank of pebbles, traces of a submerged forest can sometimes be seen at low tide.

🚗 SAUNDERSFOOT, on the B4316, is 3 miles north of Tenby.

SCOLTON MANOR COUNTRY PARK
Dyfed

A neat Georgian mansion is the centrepiece of this small but wide-ranging country park. Within a 40-acre estate, Scolton Manor embraces everything from prehistory to the Age of Steam, specimen trees to butterflies.

The house, built in 1840, looks down onto landscaped grounds and spruce and fir plantations, deciduous trees and a 19th-century aboretum with exotic specimens which are only now reaching full maturity. The estate also has a butterfly garden and small pond.

Museum displays and exhibition material are shared amongst a number of buildings. The manor house preserves its period décor, whilst the stables to the rear feature rural crafts. A purpose built exhibition hall, next to these outbuildings, focuses on Pembrokeshire's past from prehistoric to medieval times. Out-of-doors, the old county's 19th-century railway history is represented by Margaret, a brightly painted saddle tank steam locomotive.

🚗 SCOLTON MANOR is on the B4329, 5 miles north-east of Haverfordwest.

SKOMER, SKOKHOLM AND GRASSHOLM ISLANDS
Dyfed

This foreign-sounding trio of islands remind us of another turbulent chapter in Welsh history. Their Norse-inspired names have been handed down from the Vikings, a brilliant but bellicose sea-faring race who terrorized the shores of Wales between the 9th and 11th centuries.

Today's island invaders are of the feathered, air-borne variety. The islands are now nature reserves of international significance by virtue of their thriving colonies of sea-birds. Skomer, the largest and most accessible of the three (by day trip

St David's Cathedral, its mellow stone exterior and (above) wooden roof

from Martin's Haven in summer — see Marloes Peninsula entry) has one of the finest populations of sea-birds in north-west Europe.

The razorbill, adopted as the official symbol of the Pembrokeshire Coast National Park, breeds amongst its rocks and sea-cliffs, one of an ornothological superabundance of species that includes guillemots, puffins, fulmars, shags and Manx shearwaters. The island is also renowned for its wild flowers (try to visit it during the bluebell season), a unique type of vole and the Atlantic grey seals which bask on its reefs.

Skokholm, Britain's first bird observatory (established in 1933) supports similar colonies of birds, though this small island does not normally allow day visitors. Tiny Grassholm, 12 miles out and no more than a lone rock in the sea, is the overcrowded home of over 20,000 pairs of gannets, one of the largest colonies in the world.

🚗 *THE THREE ISLANDS are off the south-western tip of the Pembrokeshire coast.*

SOLVA
Dyfed

The quayside at Solva, snug below steep-sided slopes and a good half-mile from the open seas, is easily the safest anchorage along this part of the coast. Solva Creek, a narrow tidal inlet, completely insulates this placid little natural harbour from, in the words of an old guidebook, 'the violence of the sea' in St Bride's Bay.

In the 18th and 19th centuries, Solva was a thriving port. Limestone was brought in (the old lime kilns still line the harbourside) and agricultural produce was shipped out. People were also an important cargo in the days before good roads and railways — though the prospect of a sea-

journey from Solva to Bristol, for example, paled into insignificance in comparison to the trans-Atlantic crossings to America made from here by 19th-century emigrants for a fare of three pounds and ten shillings. Today's seafaring in Solva is on a slightly less heroic scale, confined mainly to the colourful holiday craft which fill the harbour.

Solva's prosperous shippers and merchants built the grand-looking residences and warehouses which lead from the quay. Some buildings have been tastefully renovated and now participate in Solva's new-found career as a centre for high-quality craft shops, selling such items as handmade clothes and pottery. One old building has become, of all things, a tropical butterfly farm where species from all over the world fly and breed in a cleverly created 'tropical forest' climate.

🚗 *SOLVA, on the A487, is 12 miles north-west of Haverfordwest.*

STACKPOLE HEAD AND BARAFUNDLE BAY
Dyfed

More spectacular south Pembrokeshire coastline displays

Barafundle's cliff-framed beach

itself here — though only to those prepared to use their feet. Stackpole Quay, accessible by narrow minor road, is the footpath's starting point. This well preserved little stone jetty, once a busy limestone-exporting port, lies on the northern doorstep to one of Pembrokeshire's finest beaches.

At one time, the secluded, dune-backed sands at Barafundle Bay were the private preserve of the local gentry. Nowadays, anyone who cares to walk the half-mile across the headland from Stackpole Quay can take pleasure from this lovely beach.

South of the beach, the distinctive square-ended promontory of Stackpole Head comes into view. The Pembrokeshire Coast Path between beach and headland is a must for bird-watchers, for it looks directly down on to the largest congregation of breeding sea-birds — guillemots, razorbills and kittiwakes in particular — on Pembrokeshire's mainland.

🚗 *STACKPOLE QUAY is accessible by minor road, about 4 miles south of Pembroke.*

STACK ROCKS AND ST GOVAN'S HEAD
Dyfed

The coastline south of Pembroke is not recommended for those prone to vertigo. Terra firma ends abruptly in a towering line of limestone cliffs, one of the finest in Britain, populated by teeming colonies of sea-birds.

The strangely-named Elegug Stacks, or Stack Rocks, bear dramatic witness to the action of the waves. This massive pair of limestone pillars, cast adrift from the land by the destructive forces of the sea, are remnants of a collapsed sea-cave. At

Right: **Snug St Govan's Chapel, huddled in the base of the cliffs**

Stack Rocks, land lost to the sea and sea-birds

Georgian elegance in aspic at Tenby harbour

one time, they probably resembled the nearby 'Green Bridge of Wales,' a magnificent natural sea-arch and probably the most celebrated sight on the south Pembrokeshire coast.

Just over three miles to the south east are the magnificent rocks and headlands at St Govan's Head. Huddled in the base of the cliffs, and accessible by 52 stone steps, is the minute St Govan's Chapel. This ancient chapel, almost undetectable in its deep, shady gorge, has been a place of pilgrimage since medieval time.

🚗 *THIS PART OF THE COAST is accessible by minor roads off the B4319 south of Pembroke (please note that this is a Ministry of Defence area, and public access is sometimes restricted).*

TENBY
Dyfed

Not often, hand-on-heart, can a popular seaside resort be described as possessing dignity and understated

charm. Tenby is one of those rare exceptions. Its beaches, harbour and town are busy enough — the latter, a maze of narrow medieval streets, seems purpose-built to encourage traffic jams. Yet Tenby manages to take it all in its stride without making any of the garish concessions to change seen all too often along the British coast.

The Victorian description of Tenby (a resort 'whose every view is picturesque in the extreme') is current today. Tenby's harbour, for example, is pure picture-book. Pastel-shaded Georgian houses rise in harmonious ranks above the quayside. Sheer cliffs, lined with hotels, gaze down onto two attractive beaches. The old town is full of interesting nooks and crannies, including the Tudor Merchant's House, a relic of Tenby's prosperous seafaring days. The Five Arches gateway guards an entrance in the well-preserved town walls, Tenby's greatest medieval remains and the most complete circuit in South Wales.

Nowadays, Tenby's fishermen also rely on tourism. In summer, the waters off Tenby are busy with boats carrying visitors the two miles to Caldey Island. *Caldey* is Norse for 'cold', Viking plunderers naming this island possibly after an uncomfortable winter visit when the wind whips wickedly across from the west. On a summer's day, Caldey is balmy and beautiful. Most visitors make for the monastery, where the monks produce a famous range of

perfumes made from its island's flower petals.

Caldey has been a sanctuary for religious men since the 6th century. Old priory buildings and a lovely 13th-century church mark the site of the island's original monastic settlement. Today, the monks live in an abbey built early this century, open to the public, or half of it, (men only), on conducted tours.

🚗 *TENBY is on the A478, 27 miles south-west of Carmarthen.*

The Landsker

It is no exaggeration to claim that south and north Pembrokeshire are as different as chalk and cheese. Tenby is the centre of an area known as 'the little England beyond Wales'. South Pembrokeshire is dotted with villages — Templeton, Rosemarket and Cheriton East to name but a few — bearing names which would appear to be more at home on a map of southern England. Only in the north of Pembrokeshire does the 'Welshry' reassert itself with placenames like Maenclochog and Llandysilio.

The reason behind this division is a deep and sometimes disputed one. Its mystique is multiplied by the fact that the line which divides north and south — the landsker or 'land-scar' — is a ghostly barrier which appears on no official map. Although ephemeral in the cartographic sense, its on-the-ground actuality is real enough.

The landsker runs across country from Amroth in the south to Newgale on the west coast, its course marked by a series of castles such as Llawhaden, Narberth and Roch. According to most experts, these castles are the key element in understanding the split between 'Englishry' and 'Welshry'. In the 11th and 12th centuries, the invading Normans established this frontier of castles, behind which the Welsh retreated. In their wake came Anglo-Saxon and Flemish immigrants and a 'little England' of imported ways, customs, farming methods, architecture and alien placenames.

Villages facing each other on either side of the line once had little in common with each other. Welsh-speaking and traditional chapel-going communities would have nothing to do with their English-speaking Anglican neighbours, and vice-versa. Intermarriage was, of course, unthinkable.

In recent times, the landsker's relevance has inevitably declined though its presence can still be felt. This lingering influence may lend credence to the alternative — and altogether more atavistic interpretation placed upon it.

North Pembrokeshire's underlying rocks, rugged and resilient, are amongst the oldest in the British Isles. The rocks in the south, by comparison, are much younger and softer. This immutable difference between north and south prompts romantics to claim that the landsker is some kind of cultural manifestation which reflects man's deep-rooted relationship with the earth on which he stands.

A Norman frontier or mystical measure of man's nature? Take your pick.

Llawhaden Castle, shell-like guardian of the ghostly landsker

Non-Welsh Wales — a Flemish chimney at St Florence

51

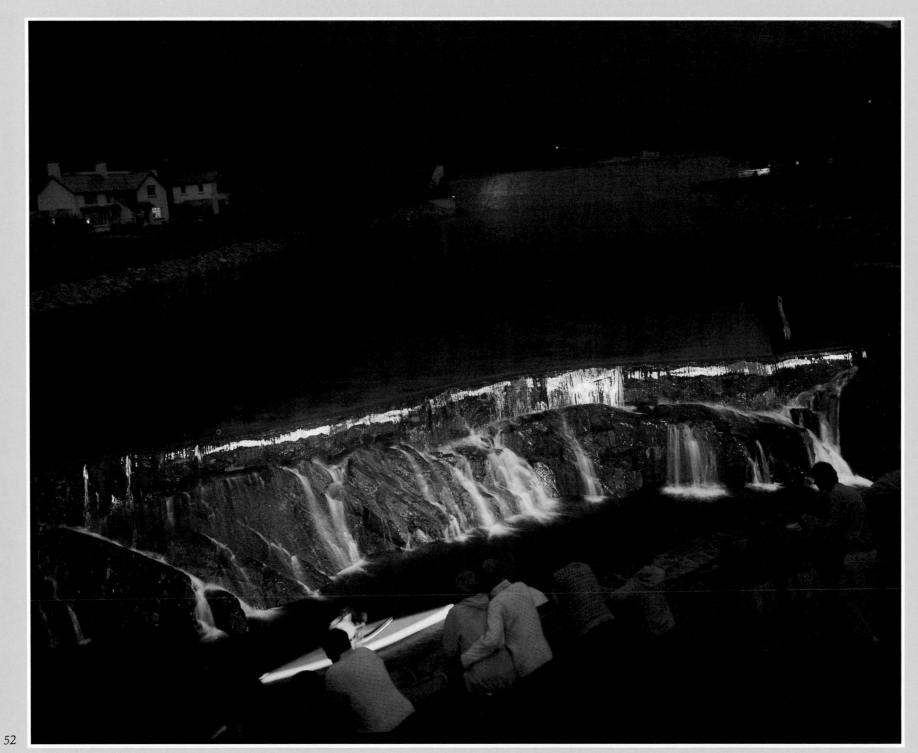

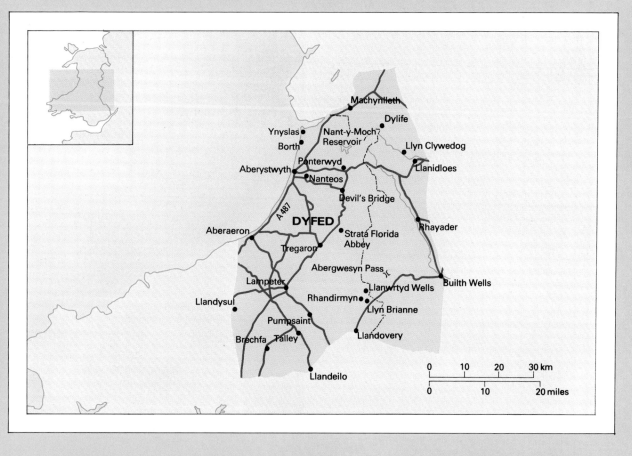

The River Rheidol rushes over falls floodlit on summer nights. Born in the inhospitable Plynlimon Mountains, its waters have been dammed to generate hydro-electricity

EORGE BORROW, a mid-19th-century writer and traveller, recorded his impressions of a journey through Wales in a work which has since become a classic. In naming his book *Wild Wales* he captured, at a stroke, the powerful and sometimes savage personality of the Welsh hills and mountains. Were he to retrace his steps today in search of the 19th-century scenes he wrote so vividly about, he would be drawn to this area, the Wales of his 'wildest solitudes'.

Change continues to be determined by the cycle of the seasons in the Welsh heartlands. Admittedly, the hand of man makes its presence felt — since Borrow's time, for example, massive lakelands and substantial conifer forests have been created. But Mid Wales's tenacious hill-sheep farmers are still here in highlands that remain largely inviolate.

The Cambrian Mountains, the 'backbone of Wales', fill much of these heartlands. There are no great peaks as in the north; rather a large, empty and consistently high upland region of moors, plateaux and rolling mountain crests which reveal their innermost secrets only to those on foot or horseback. Four-wheel exploration is confined to the few narrow mountain roads which gingerly traverse this difficult terrain.

These are the Welsh heartlands in more than a geographic sense. Not surprisingly, they have successfully rebuffed outside influences over the centuries — Roman and Norman invaders made little headway — and survive as a stronghold of Welsh customs and traditions.

53

ABERAERON
Dyfed

Aberaeron's Georgian harbourside is a gem. The most incompetent of photographers would be hard-pressed to come away with an undistinguished picture of this quayside, lined as it is by buildings which express the essential elements of Georgian architecture in their harmonious proportions, consistency of line and pared-down elegance.

This attractive sea-town owes its good looks to the fact that it was purpose-built to a set plan as a port in the 19th century. Aberaeron flourished as a fishing and trading port and shipbuilding centre during Cardigan Bay's great seafaring days. The death knell was sounded by the coming of the railways, and Aberaeron built its last boat in 1884.

The boats are back now, for Aberaeron has become a popular holiday sailing centre. Aberaeron Sea Aquarium, on the harbourside, gives visitors an insight into the marine life to be found off the west coast of Wales.

🚗 *ABERAERON is at the junction of the A487 and A482, 16 miles south-west of Aberystwyth.*

ABERGWESYN PASS
Dyfed and Powys

George Borrow's classic 19th-century travel book, *Wild Wales*, embodied in its title the uncompromising terrain of the Welsh uplands. He tramped across many a lonely moorland the length and breadth of Wales, so when he found 'some of the wildest solitudes' near Tregaron his assessment deserves to be taken seriously.

So too does the narrow ribbon of tarmac that ventures tenuously into the wilderness from Tregaron. This is the Abergwesyn Pass, one of the few genuinely stimulating motoring experiences left in Britain today. The road follows the course of an old drovers' route across a desolate, uninhabited and unforgettably beautiful landscape of high moorland and rolling mountain crests, passing along the way nothing more than the occasional isolated farmstead and reassuring red telephone box.

For 14 miles and countless curves it weaves its way over an area variously described as the 'roof of Wales' or 'great Welsh desert', descending the hairpinned Devil's Staircase to the hamlet of Abergwesyn and the return of civilization. Just over half-way along, the pass is linked by a new road to the Llyn Brianne reservoir (see separate entry).

🚗 *THE ABERGWESYN PASS can be approached from the west via Tregaron, from the south-east via Llanwrtyd Wells and Abergwesyn.*

ABERYSTWYTH
Dyfed

Although strictly an unofficial title, Aberystwyth is regarded by most as the 'capital' of Mid Wales. This large town, right in the middle of Cardigan Bay, combines three roles with commendable aplomb: those of a seaside resort, university campus and main shopping and administrative centre, with a population of over 12,000, along the bay.

To the Victorian traveller, Aberystwyth was the fashionable 'Biarritz of Wales' which 'seems to scorn the novelties which find favour in the newer and more frivolous watering places'. This description more or less stands today, for Aberystwyth is not a town to move with the times.

Its long, curving promenade, with a ruined medieval castle at one end and a grey-rocked headland at the

Four miles-per-hour mountaineering on Aberystwyth's Cliff Railway

other, is formal and dignified. The ambience of the Victorian Age extends to the 430-ft summit of the headland itself, known as Constitution Hill. It is scaled by a cliff railway, the only one in Wales and a 'conveyance of gentlefolk since 1896'. A camera obscura has recently been installed on the summit to exploit the wide views. This re-creation of a popular Victorian amusement is equipped with a huge 14-inch lens (the biggest in the world, they claim) which captures all of Cardigan Bay and no less than 26 mountain peaks.

The hillsides above the beach are occupied by the large university campus and National Library of Wales, an important Welsh institution which contains many of the oldest documents and books in the Welsh language. The Ceredigion Museum, in the town itself, is well worth a visit. Coastal and rural history and traditions are recalled here, though the star of the show is the museum building itself, an ornate Edwardian music hall. There are more links with the past at Aberystwyth's railway station, the terminus of the Vale of

Rheidol narrow-gauge railway, British Rail's last remaining operational link with the Age of Steam, which chuffs along a 12-mile route to Devil's Bridge.

Llanbadarn Fawr, now a suburb of Aberystwyth, is the home of a grand 12th-century church, one of the largest in Wales, its surprising stature a reflection of the influential role this site has played in religious history since the 6th century.

ABERYSTWYTH is accessible by the A487 from the south and north, the A44 and A4120 from the east.

BORTH AND YNYSLAS
Dyfed

The small stretch of Cardigan Bay between Borth and Ynyslas, its hinterland uncharacteristically as flat as a pancake, is sandy, windswept, and mostly silent. From Borth — a long, straggling and undistinguished little seaside resort — the scenery improves immeasurably.

The dunes and vast expanses of low-tide sands north of Ynyslas command magnificent views across the Dyfi estuary to the mountains around Machynlleth. Aberdovey, on the opposite bank, appears as a brightly-painted dividing line between sandy shore and steep green hillside. The Dyfi estuary's dunes and salt marshes are an important habitat for birds, butterflies and unusual plants. An information centre (open summer only) serves as an introduction to the large area around Ynyslas which is protected as a nature reserve.

BORTH, 6 miles north of Aberystwyth, is accessible by the B4572 or B4353 off the A487 (same directions apply in Ynyslas, 2 miles north of Borth).

BRECHFA
Dyfed

This small village gives its name to one of the largest man-made forests in Wales. The conifers of the Brechfa Forest march in orderly ranks above the village and across a high plateau almost all the way to Llanybydder, nine miles to the north.

Tiny Brechfa is not completely crowded out by all these trees. The views to the south, across the fast-flowing River Marlais, are of open, green and pleasant hill country. The Marlais, and the nearby Cothi into which it flows, help explain Brechfa's popularity, for both rivers are noted for their salmon and sewin (Welsh for sea-trout).

Brechfa, almost sealed off in the back lanes, also attracts those in search of undiluted peace and quiet. Some visitors choose to stay in its 16th-century manor house, Ty Mawr ('The Big House'), which has been converted into an intimate little hotel. The Brechfa Forest to the north is not as inhospitable as it might first sound. Waymarked footpaths and picnic areas sited around its fringes (Brechfa's neighbouring village of Abergorlech is particularly well-endowed) encourage exploration of this vast woodland.

BRECHFA is on the B4310, 12 miles north-east of Carmarthen.

BUILTH WELLS
Powys

Builth's days as a spa resort may be long gone, but its status as a country and farming town is more assured than ever. The markets held here each Monday are important enough locally, though they are put in the shade by the one event entered in the diaries of all countrymen and women: the Royal Welsh Agricultural Show, held

The Ceredigion Museum

here over four days each July, an occasion which attracts farming folk — and urbanites interested in country pursuits — from all over Wales.

Grey-stoned Builth, properly traditional in character, has a fine, six-arched bridge across the River Wye, a pleasant tree-lined riverside promenade, and scant ruins of a medieval castle. The one exuberant touch is provided by the Wyeside Arts Centre, a renovated red-bricked building based around the old cinema and basement market hall.

Cilmeri, three miles west of Builth, is a place familiar to all students of Welsh history. A roadside monument marks the spot where Llywelyn, last of the native Welsh princes, was killed by an English trooper during a chance encounter in 1282.

🚗 *BUILTH is at the junction of the A470 and A483 between Brecon and Rhayader.*

DEVIL'S BRIDGE
Dyfed

The locals living in this dramatically-named mountain village are becoming a little tired of the jokey question: 'Where the devil is the bridge?' In fact, there are three bridges in all, one piled on top of the next, well camouflaged amongst thick woods in a deep and gloomy gorge.

The oldest, *Pont-y-gwr Drwy* ('The Bridge of the Evil One', its name deriving from a devilish folk tale), is the lowest, a simple stone arch across the narrow ravine. A second, wider bridge, put up in 1708, is sandwiched between this original medieval crossing point and a 'new' iron bridge, constructed in 1901, which still carries road traffic.

Devil's Bridge is perched on the flanks of the Plynlimon mountains. Views from the terrace in front of the Hafod Arms (which, thanks to its gabled roof and huge eaves, would look more at home in an alpine ski resort than in the middle of Wales) are splendid.

Most visitors come, though, for what lies down below in William Wordsworth's 'dread chasm', accessible by a precipitious staircase footpath, where the River Mynach plunges 300 ft in a series of torrents on the way to its confluence with the River Rheidol.

The Rheidol has carved a steep and spectacular valley for itself as it winds its way to the sea at Aberystwyth. The Vale of Rheidol narrow-gauge railway, one of the 'Great Little Trains of Wales', gazes down onto the river from a lofty ledge cut into the mountainside. Along its scenic 12-mile route from Aberystwyth to Devil's Bridge, the Rheidol Falls come into view far below, next to the Cwm Rheidol hydro-electric power station (open to visitors in summer).

🚗 *DEVIL'S BRIDGE, at the junction of the A4120, B4343 and B4574, is 12 miles east of Aberystwyth.*

DYLIFE
Powys

High, lonely, desolate Dylife is an eerie sight, especially when it looms unexpectedly into view out of the mists. Mountain moor has been

Amid rugged countryside near Devil's Bridge, the Cwm Rheidol hydro-electric scheme flourishes

scoured away or buried by lead-waste from a great mining settlement, the grey surface remains of which create a lunar-like landscape. Between the 1770s and 1896, when the mines were abandoned, armies of workmen were attracted to this isolated, inhospitable spot. One wonders where they all lived, for Dylife today is nothing more than a few farms and one pub.

Ffrwd Fawr, one of the highest waterfalls in Wales, plunges down a lovely, sheltered valley tucked in below the road on the eastern approach to Dylife. West of the settlement, the mountains proper take over. From Dylife, the road — another of Wales's truly exhilarating mountain passes — climbs to a summit of 1671 ft before beginning its long descent across sharp crests down into the Dulas Valley and Machynlleth.

🚗 *DYLIFE is on a minor road, accessible either from Machynlleth or off the B4518, 12 miles north west of Llanidloes.*

LAMPETER
Dyfed

This town, large by Teifiside standards, is a busy meeting place of routes and an important seat of learning. A pleasant mix of Georgian and Victorian buildings fan out with the roads in all directions from the centre of town. The University College of St David's, one of the seven branches of the University of Wales (Cardiff has three and there are others in Swansea, Aberystwyth and Bangor) stands right in the centre.

The university, the second oldest in Britain after Oxford and Cambridge, was founded in 1822 as a Welsh counterpart to those august colleges. Parallels with Oxford extend to its architecture. The handsome main building, finished in Tudor style, is ranged around a quadrangle with corner towers, a fountain and clocktower.

A scruffy, heather-covered mound at the side of the college disturbs an otherwise orderly campus. It nevertheless commands respect, for it is the remnant of a medieval castle put up to defend a strategic crossing point on the Teifi.

On the last Thursday in each month, Llanybydder, a village five miles south-west of Lampeter, is transformed into an equinine mecca. Buyers from all over Britain and as far afield as the Continent come here for the famous horse fair, where hundreds of ponies and horses are sold off by rapid-fire auctioneers during hectic trading.

🚗 *LAMPETER is at the junction of the A482, A485, A475, and B4343, roughly mid-way between Llandovery and Aberaeron.*

LLANDYSUL
Dyfed

One way or another, Llandysul's livelihood has always come under the influence of the River Teifi. The river's soft waters, ideal for washing wool, also powered the waterwheels of the woollen mills which, in their heyday, turned Llandysul into the busiest weaving centre in Wales. Modest quantities of this distinctive, traditionally-patterned cloth are still produced locally (see Maesllyn Woollen Mill entry), though the boom years have long since passed.

The Teifi now attracts anglers and canoeists to the town. Fishing for salmon and sea-trout is excellent, whilst white-water canoeists take up the challenge of an exciting slalom course as the Teifi tumbles through a narrow, rocky course beneath the river bridge.

Haste is replaced by repose a short distance upstream. Here, the Teifi charts a slow and gentle course past Llandysul's most imposing historic site. This is the splendid Church of St Tysul, a large 13th-century affair with a fine castellated tower. Llandysul itself, rising in a series of steep terraces above church and river, is a businesslike little country and market town in which sheep and cattle sales are still held once a fortnight.

🚗 *LLANDYSUL is at the junction of the A486, B4336 and B4476, 16 miles north of Carmarthen, 12 miles south-west of Lampeter.*

LLANIDLOES
Powys

Based on the sole criteria of a central location, Llanidloes would easily qualify as the capital of Wales. Sited right in the middle of Mid Wales, this pretty little town is equidistant from north and south.

Llanidloes is a meeting place of infuences, poised between the traditional stone-built farmsteads of the Welsh hills and the striking black-and-white architecture typical of the border country. The town's old market hall belongs to the latter category. This late-16th-century building, the only one of its kind surviving in Wales, is eye catching in the extreme. Built in half-timbered, black-and-white style, it stands on hefty timber piers above an open market place right in the middle of town, the perfect Elizabethan traffic bottleneck.

Its upper storey now houses the local museum, which reflects Llanidloes's surprisingly rumbustious past as a 19th-century textile town and scene of Chartist riots. The existence in Llanidloes of one of the late Laura Ashley's worldwide chain of fabric shops also comes as something of a surprise to those unaware that the company's factory is located at nearby Carno.

🚗 *LLANIDLOES, at the junction of the A470, B4518 and B4569, is 28 miles east of Aberystwyth.*

Inspecting the goods at Llanybydder horse fair

Welsh Woollens

Any traveller passing through the green heartlands of Mid Wales will soon become aware that sheep outnumber people quite conclusively. At one time, the ratio was put even higher than the current three-to-one; little wonder, then, that so much surplus fleece stimulated cloth making in Wales, a tradition almost 2000 years old.

Throughout the centuries, and up to quite recent times, woollen weaving has been one of Wales's most important industries. 'Industry' is perhaps a misleading term to use when describing its early days. Cloth weaving was originally a domestic activity. Most small farmers were growers, spinners and weavers, making their own cloth from spinning wheels and weaving looms.

The transition from hand spinning and weaving to powered machinery came after the Middle Ages. A previously scattered 'cottage industry' became concentrated firstly within small riverbank mills powered by waterwheel and later, with the Industrial Revolution in full swing, highly organised and mechanised factories.

Celtic designs and bold colours are characteristics of Welsh woollens

Woollen mills still produce traditional Welsh weaves

As the industry developed, its focal point shifted around Wales. In the Middle Ages, Pembrokeshire's cottage industries were pre-eminent. By the mid 18th century, Mid Wales had developed as a thriving flannel manufacturing centre, with towns such as Llanidloes and Newtown — the latter known as 'the Leeds of Wales' — almost entirely dependent on textile production. By the late 19th century, the Teifi Valley had taken over. At Drefach Felindre (now the home of the Museum of the Welsh Woollen Industry), for example, there were no less than 52 mills in full production.

A catastrophic decline in the industry since the 1920s has left Wales with only a handful of mills, dispersed throughout the country. Most are fully mechanised, though some retain their old waterwheels in working order. Many of the mills also welcome visitors, and make special efforts to explain the evolution of the industry from the relative simplicity of the domestic spinning wheel to the complexities of the machine age.

Not that the surviving mills should be looked upon as museum pieces. Their distinctively patterned Welsh weaves, a robust interpretation of bold Celtic motifs in strong colours, are much in demand. The characteristic, typically-Welsh product is the heavy tapestry or double-woven cloth, a multi-coloured material used for bedspreads. Flannels, tweeds and blankets are also woven, and a whole range of garments made up from Welsh cloth.

LLANWRTYD WELLS
Powys

Today, it is difficult to envisage this sleepy little town as it must have been in its heyday, when steam trains and charabancs disgorged thousands of summer visitors to 'take the waters'. Llanwrtyd's sulphur, chalybeate and saline springs certainly attracted the crowds when spa holidays were fashionable, though the town's location, on the doorstep of untouched hill country, must also have contributed to its popularity.

Llanwrtyd now relies entirely on its enviable situation. The old well — the aptly named Y *Ffynnon Ddrewllyd* ('The Stinking Well') — is still there and has been partially renovated, so anyone curious enough can once again sample its foul-smelling sulphur water. Most visitors, however, prefer to confine themselves to fishing on the crystal River Irfon or to exploring the hills on horseback.

The town claims to have 'invented' pony trekking — now a popular pastime throughout Britain — in the 1950s. The surrounding terrain, unquestionably ideal for four-legged exploration, has also inspired a challenging 'Man versus Horse' marathon, held here each May. The only hint of industry in this restful place is provided by the Cambrian Woollen Factory, on the outskirts of town, where visitors are welcome to view the weaving process.

LLANWRTYD WELLS is on the A483 between Llandovery and Builth Wells.

LLYN BRIANNE
Dyfed

A helicopter ride is the only way to capture the full enormity of this man-made reservoir. Its watery tentacles extend in many directions into the folds of totally uninhabited highland, one of the last true wildernesses in Wales, north of Llandovery. Motorists have to be content with a new road, cut across previously inaccessible terrain. This follows the eastern shoreline, climbing and swooping roller-coaster fashion alongside drowned valleys before meeting up with the old drovers' route along the Abergwesyn Pass (see separate entry).

Llyn Brianne, opened in 1973, supplies Swansea with its water. A massive, rock-filled dam — the highest of its type in Britain — holds back a 13,500 million gallon lake formed by the headwaters of the Tywi and Camddwr Rivers. A path across the dam leads to the western shores, open to walkers only, where the red kite is sometimes spotted.

LLYN BRIANNE is accessible by minor road about 10 miles north of Llandovery.

LLYN CLYWEDOG
Powys

This sinuous man-made lake fills a steep-sided, six-mile-long fold in silent hill-sheep country above Llanidloes. Llyn Clywedog's 11,000 million gallons do more than supply the Midlands with water, for they also provide recreation in the form of trout fishing and sailing.

Part and parcel of its construction in the 1960s involved a ring road around its lakesides. There are panoramic viewing points along the B4518 which runs close to its eastern shores. Better still is the minor road along the western banks which leads to a viewing area overlooking the 237-ft-high concrete dam. The green hillsides near the dam provide a scenic setting for an incongruous interloper, in the form of a 19th-century industrial site. This is the Bryn Tail Lead Mine, one of the many such mines sunk in Mid Wales during the boom years over a century ago. Extraction and ore crushing took place here, on a site which is now preserved and open to the public.

LLYN CLYWEDOG is accessible by the B4518, approximately 4 miles north-west of Llanidloes.

MACHYNLLETH
Powys

All eyes are unavoidably drawn to Machynlleth's bizarre, over-ornamental clock tower, right in the centre of town, put up in 1873 by the Marquess of Londonderry. Like it or loathe it, it is quite impossible to ignore this horological embellishment which seems at odds with Machynlleth's otherwise harmonious character.

Town planners — or possibly the lack of them — have bestowed upon Machynlleth a wide main thoroughfare lined with architecturally distinguished buildings, some Georgian, others of robust local stone or striking black-and-white half-timbered construction. Such is the length and breadth of this accommodating street that it only really becomes busy when stallholders set up camp here on market day (every Wednesday), perpetuating a tradition that goes back, according to some, over 700 years.

The Owain Glyndwr Institute along the street stirs many a Welshman into historic and mythological speculation over the events of 1404 and what might have been. Owain, Wales's last native leader, held a Welsh parliament at Machynlleth, reputedly on this site. Welsh aspirations for independence disappeared along with Owain, who vanished in 1412, never to be seen again. The life of this mercurial folk-hero is remembered in the Owain Glyndwr Centre, next to the Dyfi Centre which conveys a wide range of information on the locality.

The Marquess of Londonderry lived at Plas Machynlleth, located in parkland just behind the Wynnstay Hotel, the latter's pedigree as an historic coaching inn plainly evident in its arched entrance. The Plas, a fine looking house dating from the 17th century, now serves as a rather grand centre for local government offices.

Furnace, six miles to the south-west, is named after a 17th-century silver refinery, later replaced by an early ironworks (currently under restoration). A picturesque cascade tumbles through the woods before flowing past the old foundry, its waters once turning a wheel which powered the bellows of the furnace. Inland from Furnace, this river — the Einion — rushes through a remote, wooded and lovely vale known as Artist's Valley.

MACHYNLLETH, at the junction of the A487, A489 and A493, is 18 miles north-east of Aberystwyth.

Machynlleth's eccentric clock tower keeps time for the street market

NANTEOS
Dyfed

Devotees of Georgian architecture should make every effort to visit this country house, hidden in the hills east of Aberystwyth. Not that Nanteos is a typical neat-and-tidy Georgian mansion. Its facade cannot be described as immaculate, its interior is shabby rather than showpiece.

Herein lies Nanteos's fascination and unique appeal. The house, dating from 1739, is being slowly restored after a long period of neglect. Unlike other country houses, Nanteos gives the public a sobering insight into the costly, daunting reality behind the rescue and preservation of Britain's architectural heritage. Stately homes never quite seem the same again after a trip around Nanteos.

The house boasts quite a history. The composer Richard Wagner stayed here, and up until the 1950s Nanteos claimed ownership of the Holy Grail, the cup used by Christ in the Last Supper.

NANTEOS, about 4 miles south-east of Aberystwyth, can be reached by minor road off the B4340.

NANT-Y-MOCH RESERVOIR
Dyfed

An elemental landscape of mountain wilderness and water fills the terrain to the north of Ponterwyd. The undisturbed solitudes of the Plynlimon range sweep across the skyline, though unlike conventional mountains this one fails to rise to a climactic, identifiable peak. Its 2468-ft summit is there, somewhere, amongst an outcrop of dark crags that break out from a brooding moorland dome to the east of the Nant-y-Moch reservoir.

Plynlimon, Mid Wales's central core, commands clear-day views as far as North and South Wales. The boggy walk to the top should not be undertaken lightly: most visitors to these uplands are content merely to gaze towards the summit from the mountain road that skirts the western shores of Nant-y-Moch. The inky-black waters of this 7000-million-gallon reservoir, contained by a huge buttressed dam 172-ft high across the River Rheidol, are used to provide hydro-electric power for the Central Electricity Generating Board's Cwm Rheidol scheme (see Devil's Bridge entry).

NANT-Y-MOCH is accessible by minor road off the A44 north of Ponterwyd or east off the A487 at Talybont.

PONTERWYD
Dyfed

Ponterwyd's George Borrow Hotel encapsulates the character of this isolated settlement, high in the mist-shrouded Plynlimon mountains. The hotel, re-named in honour of the 19th-century author of *Wild Wales*, was a welcome refuge to Borrow following his plod across bog and moorland.

Moorland turns into moonscape just west of the village. Grey-green scars in the landscape are the remnants of a metalliferous mining field which, in its heyday, straddled Plynlimon. At the Llywernog Silver-Lead Mine, one mile west of Ponterwyd, the mining boom years of the 1870s have been preserved for posterity. This mine, abandoned like so many others in the late 19th century, has been restored as a museum which recaptures the life and work of the Mid Wales metal miner.

Forestry is now the only 'industry' in these parts. The Bwlch Nant-yr-Arian Forest Visitor Centre, one mile west of Llywernog, gives the public an insight into the work of the Forestry Commission, which has had such a pronounced impact on the landscape in Mid Wales. The spread of the ubiquitous conifer rouses strong feelings in some, though no one can argue that the commission, in the last decade or so, has not made commendable attempts to realise the recreational value of its woodlands. Bwlch Nant-yr-Arian is a good case in point. In addition to its imaginative displays on local history and landscape, the centre — sited on a crest and commanding superb views into the valley below — is surrounded by waymarked walks and picnic areas.

PONTERWYD, at the junction of the A44 and A4120, is 12 miles east of Aberystwyth.

PUMPSAINT
Dyfed

Pumpsaint's name is bound up in a mis-shapen grey stone which stands in a shady knoll in the hills just east of the village. Assiduous visitors will count five indentations in the monolith, said to be the impressions left by the heads of five saints (*pump sant* in Welsh) who used the stone as a communal pillow.

Only the most credulous will persevere with this piece of Welsh hokum on discovering that the stone stands at the entrance to the Dolaucothi Roman Gold Mines. The alternative explanation — that the stone was simply used to pound ore — may be dull, but it has an unavoidable ring of truth about it.

Uncorroborated legend does not surround the gold mines. Dolaucothi is the only site in Britain where it has been definitely established that the Romans mined for gold. Serious mining began here in A.D. 75, Welsh

Lofty views from the Bwlch Nant-yr-Arian Forest Visitor Centre

gold swelling the coffers of the Imperial Mint at Lyons for 100 years.

Thousands of slaves were transported to this remote spot, and a camp was thrown up by the Romans (on the site of the Dolaucothi Arms in the village) to protect their investment. Yet visitors expecting to see overt evidence of this mammoth endeavour are invariably thwarted, for Dolaucothi's Roman interlude has been masked by centuries of disuse (though the site was again mined between the 1870s and 1938).

The sophistication of the Romans' mining operations becomes apparent only to those prepared to look

beyond a thick cloak of wood and bush. Faint traces remain of an incredibly complicated aqueduct system — one stretch no less than seven miles long — in the surrounding hillsides. Overgrown slopes ultimately reveal hidden tunnel entrances and the leftovers from opencast mining.

Waymarked footpaths give a reasonably good understanding of this fascinating and unique National Trust site. Better still are the summer guided tours which take in parts of the underground workings.

PUMPSAINT is on the A482 between Lampeter and Llanwrda.

RHANDIRMWYN
Dyfed

Before the opening of the Llyn Brianne reservoir in the 1970s, Rhandirmwyn was known only to the fortunate few. Up until then, this scattered village, set on a hillside overlooking the wildly beautiful Upper Tywi Valley, was at the end of the road. With the reservoir came new roads, opening up a remote corner of Wales which had previously been accessible only on foot or horseback.

Rhandirmwyn, the last outpost before the wilderness areas of Abergwesyn and the 'roof of Wales', has a surprising history. A veil of trees draws itself over abandoned levels in the mountainsides above the village, keeping secret the fact that Rhandirmwyn was once one of Europe's largest lead mining centres.

There are more secret places just north of the village. Twm Shon Catti, the Welsh Robin Hood, hid from the Sheriff of Carmarthen amongst the boulder-strewn and densely wooded upper slopes of Dinas Hill. This enigmatic 16th-century character — an out-and-out villain according to some — is generally regarded as a local hero who, in an episode reminiscent of a western movie, avoided injuring his enemy by pinning him to his saddle with a carefully placed arrow.

Twm's hiding place was a cave, in the slopes directly above a rocky gorge through which the Tywi flows with some ferocity. Our villainous hero would be gratified to learn that it is still quite difficult to find, even though now partially waymarked off the official footpath around Dinas Hill, an R.S.P.B. nature reserve.

RHANDIRMWYN is on a minor road, approximately 7 miles north of Llandovery. It is also accessible from Tregaron and the Abergwesyn Pass. 61

RHAYADER AND THE 'LAKELANDS OF MID WALES'
Powys

The market town of Rhayader stands at the gateway to Wales's first, and most famous, collection of man-made lakes. The Birmingham Corporation were responsible for the Elan Valley lakelands, a quartet of reservoirs completed in 1904 and containing over 11,000 million gallons of water between them. The lakes — Caban Coch, Garreg Ddu, Pen-y-garreg and Craig Goch — form a watery chain almost nine miles long amongst wooded hillsides and empty moorland west of Rhayader. Unlike many of the reservoirs subsequently constructed in Wales, the Elan Valley dams have a decorative turn-of-the-century elegance, their stonework blending in well with their surroundings.

Craig Goch, the northernmost dam set amongst open mountainsides, is particularly accomplished. It presents an attractive counterpoint to the starkly functional Claerwen dam, built in the 1950s to double the capacity of these lakelands. Unlike its Elan Valley neighbours, remote, four-mile-long Claerwen locks itself away from motorised traffic, the road venturing no further than its towering dam at the head of the lake.

Rhayader, on the banks of the River Wye, is a friendly country town, architecturally unremarkable apart from a neat little clock tower which presides over its busy crossroads. The town makes the most of its location. Fishermen and pony trekkers are well provided for, as are the farmers who come to town on Wednesdays for the seasonal livestock markets.

RHAYADER, at the junction of the A470, A44 and B4518, is mid-way between Builth Wells and Llanidloes. The Elan Valley and Claerwen reservoirs, a few miles west of the town, are accessible via the B4518 and minor roads.

STRATA FLORIDA ABBEY
Dyfed

White-robed Cistercian monks, sympathetic to Welsh ways and culture, were responsible for creating the 'Westminster Abbey of Wales' in the solitudes east of Pontrhydfendigaid. They arrived c.1200 at Strata Florida, its name a latinized version of the Welsh *Ystrad Fflur* ('The way of the flowers').

Their abbey soon became more than a religious centre. At the height of its importance, Strata Florida exercised great political and educational influence. Evocative fragments are all that remain of a site which has not weathered well. A mosaic tiled floor survives in the chapel, though most impressive of all is the abbey's highly decorated Romanesque arch, miraculously intact. The bleating of sheep is the only noise which disturbs this utterly tranquil spot — a familiar sound at Strata Florida, for amongst their many talents the enterprising Cistercians were innovative and successful hill-sheep farmers.

In the graveyard, one headstone decorated with an amputated leg inspires a smile. It reads: 'The left leg and part of the thigh of Henry Hughes, cooper, was cut off and intern'd here June 18th 1756.' Whatever became of the rest of Henry is open to speculation. The grave stands close to a gnarled yew tree. According to legend, it marks the resting place of Dafydd ap Gwilym, Wales's most celebrated medieval poet (c. 1320-1380).

Hidden in the lonely hills to the north-east of the abbey are the heather-fringed Teifi Pools, headwaters of one of Wales's loveliest rivers.

STRATA FLORIDA is 1 mile east of Pontrhydfendigaid, a village on the B4340 approximately 15 miles south-east of Aberystwyth.

TALLEY
Dyfed

Twin lakes, a ruined abbey and unusual village church are four good justifications for a visit to Talley. The village's lovely location amongst silent hills and unhurried farming country is a bonus for those who seek out the remains of Talley Abbey, founded here by the Premonstratensian Order in the late 12th century. One or two slender pointed archways and stretches of ruined wall are all that now survive, on an idyllic lakeside site.

The next-door Church of St Michael is thankfully intact. Those brought up on a diet of standard ecclesiastical architecture might consider this 18th-century church to have suffered something of an identity crisis. Its missing central aisle (there are two side aisles instead) and rows

Strata Florida's decorative arch frames an utterly peaceful scene

of box pews are pure chapel rather than church, more suited to a bastion of Welsh Nonconformity than an Anglican place of worship.

🚗 *TALLEY is just off the B4302, 8 miles north of Llandeilo and about 11 miles south of Lampeter.*

TREGARON
Dyfed

The scene here has not changed substantially since the times when drovers gathered in the town square, in front of the Talbot Hotel and statue of Henry Richard, local M.P. and Victorian 'apostle of peace', before setting off with their sheep and cattle to cross the daunting Abergwesyn Pass on their way to the markets of the Midlands. Greystoned Tregaron is not a pretty town. Its charm lies in its location and staunchly traditional character. Welsh is the first language in these parts, and Tregaron is a thoroughly Welsh country and market town.

It lies in a strange no-man's-land on a dividing line between farmlands and barren, unpopulated hill country. The low-lying land to the north presents a most forbidding sight, inundated as it is by the great Bog of Tregaron, the largest in Wales, consisting of mile after mile of reedy marshland.

Tregaron Bog is a prime — and rare — example of a dome-shaped raised peat bog. This watery expanse, now a nature reserve, supports a wide variety of plants and over 40 species of breeding birds. An abandoned section of railway line running parallel to the B4343 along the eastern rim of the bog is open to the public as a nature trail which leads to a bird observation post.

🚗 *TREGARON, at the junction of the A485 and B4343, is 11 miles north-east of Lampeter.*

The remains of 12th-century Talley Abbey, idyllically situated beside twin lakes deep in Dyfed's hills

64

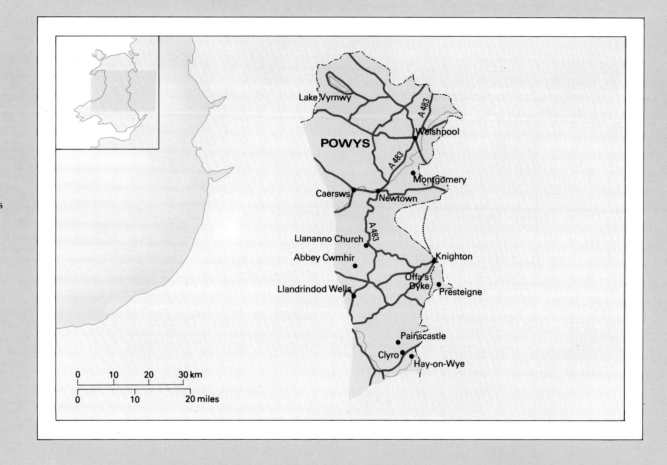

Lake Vyrnwy

A 483

Welshpool

A 483

Montgomery

Caersws

Newtown

Llananno Church

A 483

Abbey Cwmhir

Knighton

Offa's Dyke

Llandrindod Wells

Presteigne

Painscastle

Clyro

Hay-on-Wye

0   10   20   30 km

0   10   20 miles

Rood carving at its most difficult best is seen on this exquisite screen in Llananno Church

*T*RAVELLERS TEND TO pass across this lush landscape on their comings and goings through Wales, rarely stopping to aquaint themselves with its subtle, secretive charactistics. Mid Wales border country is sleepy and entirely content in its obscurity. There are no tourist honeypots here; the locals remain tight-lipped, in a take-us-or-leave-us way, about its hidden charms.

When they do speak — especially in the old county of Radnorshire (a victim of 1974's government re-organisation) — the accent is hardly Welsh. Cross-border customs and influences play a big part here. The dialect is a hybrid, rustic one, as is the architecture of the borders.

This part of Wales is famous for the half-timbered black-and-white style of building which normally typifies the English country village. Striking 'magpie' farmsteads and cottages stand out against the greenery, in complete contrast to the sturdy, stone-built dwellings of the Welsh heartlands further west.

Historically, this border country was an uneasy interface in the tensions and conflicts between Wales and England. The Offa's Dyke earthwork, a barrier created in the 8th century as the first official demarcation line between Wales and England, lies across the oscillating contours of the land like a giant, slumbering snake. Sentinel-like castles at strategic sites such as Montgomery and Welshpool survey a peaceful patchwork of farmlands that once witnessed bloody conflict.

ABBEY CWMHIR
Powys

Fragments of a Cistercian abbey reveal themselves to those who seek out this remote hamlet, tucked away amongst shady, steep hillsides north of Llandrindod Wells. Abbey Cwmhir makes up in atmosphere for what it lacks in architecture. Crumbling sections of wall and nave, hidden amongst foliage and fields beside the rushing Clywedog Brook, are all that remain of a once-thriving Cistercian house founded in 1143 — sad, really, for Abbey Cwmhir had the largest church in Wales.

Abbey Cwmhir inspires more sad reflections. It is said to be the resting place of Llywelyn, the much-lamented last native prince of Wales, whose body was brought here from Cilmeri for burial following his death in 1282 at the hands of an English trooper (see Builth Wells entry).

Following the Reformation and Dissolution of the Monasteries in 1536 the abbey was dismantled. Some of its pillars were transported to Llanidloes Church where they can still be seen today.

🚗 *ABBEY CWMHIR, 8 miles north of Llandrindod Wells, can be reached by minor road off the A483.*

BWLCH-Y-GROES PASS
Powys and Gwynedd

This spectacular mountain pass could quite as legitimately appear in the Snowdonia section of the book, for it straddles our chosen dividing line between border country and mountain. Intrepid motorists with a penchant for heights, drops and inclines together with a disregard for the narrowness of the road are strongly advised to give this exciting route a try.

Bwlch-y-Groes can be approached from three directions: via mountain-locked Lake Vyrnwy in the east, from Llanuwchllyn in the north and Dinas Mawddwy in the south-west. These three routes eventually meet at the loneliest and quietest Welsh crossroads near a 1790-ft summit which bestows on Bwlch-y-Groes the supreme title of the highest driveable mountain pass in Wales. Views from the top, which visitors share only with bemused Welsh mountain sheep, are predictably panoramic, extending to the North Wales peaks.

🚗 *BWLCH-Y-GROES is accessible off the B4393 (Lake Vyrnwy), A494 (Llanuwchllyn) or A470 (Dinas Mawddwy).*

CAERSWS
Powys

Maesmawr Hall is easy to find. This black-and-white Elizabethan house — one of the finest timber-framed buildings in Wales, and now an hotel — stands out amongst lush greenery on the banks of the meandering River Severn on the outskirts of Caersws.

Caersws's real history is a little more veiled. Almost 2000 years ago, this small village was a place of considerable importance. The Romans sited a seven-acre fort here which became a busy military crossroads, linking their power base in Chester with outposts in Mid Wales. Earthwork defences can still clearly be seen around the railway station.

Llandinam, two miles to the south, is the home of Wales's archetypal local-boy-made-good. A statue of David Davies (1818-90) by Sir Alfred Gilbert, sculptor of Piccadilly's *Eros*, stands in a pretty riverside spot in memory of the deeply religious local farmer's son who made his fortune from South Wales's mines and docks.

🚗 *CAERSWS is close to the junction of the A470 and A492, 5 miles west of Newtown.*

CLYRO
Powys

Readers of Kilvert's Diaries will immediately feel at home in the lush landscape around Clyro. From 1865 to 1872, Francis Kilvert was the curate at Clyro. His best-selling diaries, which start with the last two years of his residence here, paint a marvellous picture of life in rural Wales. Times may have changed; the village, and its surroundings, are little altered.

Peaceful Clyro, which enjoys wide views of the brooding Black Mountains, makes only a few concessions to those in search of Kilvert memorabilia. One house displays a plaque honouring the 'priest and diarist' who lodged there, and the church contains a memorial to its celebrated curate.

The Wye charts a languorous course through a broad river valley south-west of the village, flowing close to a spot with different religious associations. The Anglicanism preached by Kilvert would not have struck a chord with the religious dissenters who, under the cover of darkness, would meet at Maesyronnen, a tiny, secluded chapel tucked away on a country lane in the hillsides above the Wye.

Maesyronnen, a birthplace of the Welsh Nonconformist movement, is one of the earliest chapels in Wales. Built around 1696 and still in regular use, this humble stone house, ordinary enough from the outside, preserves a remarkable interior with original furniture — box pews, pulpit and tables — of the 18th and 19th centuries.

🚗 *CLYRO is at the junction of the A483 and B4351 between Brecon and Hereford. Maesyronnen is accessible by minor road off the A438, 3 miles south-west of Clyro.*

KNIGHTON
Powys

Much is revealed in Knighton's Welsh name, *Tref-y-Clawdd*, 'The town on the Dyke'. The dyke in question is the great north-south earthen barrier, constructed by King Offa of Mercia in the 8th century as the first official border between England and Wales (see special feature, page 71).

Knighton and the dyke are inexorably linked. The town is the only one to stand squarely on this ancient border, some of the best preserved earthworks of which can be seen in the untravelled hill country a few miles to the north-west of Knighton. Located roughly at the half-way point of the long-distance 170-mile footpath which follows the line of these earthworks, Knighton is also the natural base for the Offa's Dyke Information Centre.

The line of the Wales-England border has not changed too much since Offa's time. Visitors arriving at Knighton by train disembark in England, walking from the railway station across the bridge over the River Teme into Wales and the middle of town. Knighton's centrepiece is a 19th-century clocktower, standing amongst steep streets lined with a jumbled mixture of buildings where black-and-white 'magpie' borderland influences merge with Victorian gables.

🚗 *KNIGHTON, at the junction of the A488, A4113 and B4355, is about 19 miles north-east of Llandrindod Wells.*

LAKE VYRNWY
Powys

Vyrnwy looks like no other Welsh lake. Tall, deep-green pines encircle its shores. High mountains cocoon it from the outside world, shutting out

the sun. A spooky Gothic water tower adds the final forbidding touch to a lake that would be more at home in Switzerland or even Transylvania.

The twin-spired tower along its eastern shore gives the game away. Lake Vyrnwy is man-made, the work of the Liverpool Corporation at the end of the 19th century, a heady time when the creation of reservoirs and the indulgence of architectural eccentricity — such as the ornate water tower — were not viewed as being incompatible by the cost accountants.

Vyrnwy's tall dam holds back over 13,000 million gallons of water, still and black in its mountain shade. The village of Llanddwyn, scattered loosely about the foot of the dam, replaces the original settlement, its 37 dwellings now submerged by the four-mile long lake.

A narrow road curls around the hill immediately to the east of the dam, past the Church of St Wddyn — built to replace the old drowned church — to a wooded glade. Up amongst the trees stands a plain, grey-stoned obelisk, a sombre memorial to the 44 men who died, by accident or natural cause, during the dam's construction.

A mixture of conifer and deciduous woodland surrounds the lake. These forests are noted for their wildlife, especially birds (there is an R.S.P.B. reserve here). The lakeside fauna and the history of the reservoir are both featured at the Vyrnwy Visitor Centre in a converted chapel just west of the dam.

LAKE VYRNWY, approximately 19 miles north-west of Welshpool, is accessible by the B4393 and B4396 from the east, and narrow mountain roads from the north and west.

Lake Vyrnwy brightens its forbidding, gloomy face only when the sun shines directly overhead

LLANANNO CHURCH
Powys

Motorists speeding by on the well-engineered A483 at Llanbister between Llandrindod Wells and Newtown miss a real treat. The roadside church, situated on the banks of the River Ithon in a lovely stretch of the valley, contains what is claimed to be 'the most ornate rood screen in Wales'.

The title is justified. This rich and intricate oak screen, positioned imposingly above aisle and altar, is a supreme example of the skills displayed by the ecclesiastical woodcarver. Dating from the late 15th/early 16th century, with later additions, it embodies a wealth of breathtaking detail. Almost every square inch is redolent of patient and painstaking artistry. Leaf patterns, fruit and vine motifs — vines representing life, pomegranates death — mix and interweave in a complex pattern around a series of 25 biblical figures standing shoulder-to-shoulder.

LLANANNO CHURCH, approximately 11 miles north of Llandrindod Wells and 17 miles south of Newtown, is just over 1 mile northwest of Llanbister.

LLANDRINDOD WELLS
Powys

Unlike the other spa towns of Mid Wales, Llandrindod Wells's *belle époque* lingers quite convincingly and charmingly. Canopied shopping streets and cavernous gabled residences, a subdued riot of red and yellow-bricked Victoriana enlivened by decorative ironwork, are thoroughly busy. There is no hint of disuse or desertion here, thanks largely to the town's twin roles as the main administrative centre for the huge county of Powys and its continued

Llandrindod returns to its roots during its annual Victorian Week

popularity with visitors.

Today's guests come for the surroundings rather than the spa waters. Llandrindod Wells (shortened to a much more convenient 'Llandod' by the locals) nevertheless makes every effort to preserve, and sometimes relive, its past. For seven days each September, the town turns the clock back 100 years during its Victorian Festival. The old pump room in the 18-acre Rock Park has also been re-opened for those partial to 'taking the waters', a taste experience not as innocuous as it might sound.

Llandrindod's wealth of parklands, uniformity of architecture, boating lake and well-planned, spacious streets are no happy accident. Following the coming of the railway in 1865, it was purpose-built as Wales's premier spa resort. An exhibition cen-

tre, also in the refurbished pump rooms, captures Llandrindod's heyday and — to quote an advertisement of the times — its qualities as a 'Famous Spa . . . 750 ft above sea level. Sheltered from east winds. The splendid, bracing air, and the saline, sulphur, magnesian and chalybeate waters are very efficacious in the treatment of gout, rheumatism, anaemia, neurasthemia, dyspepsia, diabetes and liver affections.'

There is another fascinating, albeit unofficial, museum in the flamboyantly-named Automobile Palace, a town-centre garage that houses a collection of old bicycles — including penny-farthings — next to shining new cars.

LLANDRINDOD, on the junction of the A483 and A4081, is 28 miles south of Newtown.

MONTGOMERY
Powys

The gnarled shell of Montgomery Castle, high on its rocky ridge, looks directly down into a most attractive Georgian square. Mangled medieval military architecture and pristine red-bricked Georgian facades somehow sit well together in this strategic border settlement, officially a town thanks to its charter of 1227, though physically no larger than a village.

The castle's ruinous state is attributable more to the destructive forces of man rather than the elements. Much-besieged Montgomery stands guard over the Severn Valley as it enters the Welsh hills, a key position which attracted the attentions of military men for many centuries.

It was built as a front-line fortress by Henry III between 1223 and 1234. In later, more peaceful times, the castle mellowed into a manorial rather than military role, though was back in the wars again — the Civil Wars this time — in the 1640s, after which it was demolished. Thankfully, destruction was not total. A large twin-towered gatehouse, one of the earliest in Britain, massive rock-cut ditch and 220-ft deep well can still be seen, along with far-reaching views into both Wales and England.

🚗 *MONTGOMERY, at the junction of the B4385, B4386 and B4388, is 8 miles north-east of Newtown.*

NEWTOWN
Powys

By Mid Wales standards, this is a large town. It is also something of an odd-man-out, for unlike its neighbours it has a pronounced industrial history. Newtown's last years as a simple market and country town were in the 18th century. By the 19th century, it was known as 'the Leeds of Wales', a reputation based on its thriving flannel industry. Welsh flannel became the basis for the world's first mail-order business, started here in 1859, a profitable diversification which is still going strong. Today, modern estates on the outskirts of town attract new industry, bringing much-needed employment to an essentially rural area.

Newtown sits in a green basin surrounded by low hills, the town centre retaining a pleasant country air. Broad Street, a wide thoroughfare leading to a bridge across the River Severn, is particularly attractive, as are the town's riverside promenades. A former weaving workshop now serves as a textile museum which displays mill machinery, 19th-century handlooms and examples of

Robert Owen is immortalised in stone at Newtown, Powys

the cloth which made Newtown famous.

The old churchyard by the river contains the grave of Newtown's most celebrated son, Robert Owen (1771-1858). Owen, an Utopian Socialist, pioneer of factory reform and founder of the Co-operative movement, was in the vanguard of social reform in Britain. No idealistic dreamer, he put many of his egalitarian theories into practice, most notably at the New Lanark Mills in Scotland. Although he left Newtown when only a boy, he returned here towards the end of his life.

Some of Wales's most enchanting and unexplored border country lies a few miles south-east of Newtown. Around the village of Kerry, hum-mocky hills and forests, rich in prehistoric earthworks and ancient hill forts, tumble eastwards into England.

🚗 *NEWTOWN is at the junction of the A483 and A489, 13 miles south-west of Welshpool and 28 miles north of Llandrindod Wells.*

PAINSCASTLE
Powys

Aficionados of the contentedly obscure and resolutely rural will find this tiny borderland village enchanting. Do not bring any great expectations to Painscastle. The village's name says it all: castle apart, it lacks almost anything of real note.

In complete character with the place, little is left even of the castle.

Norman nobleman Pain Fitz-John erected the original earthen motte here in 1130, a makeshift stronghold rebuilt in stone by Henry III one century later. This border fort, scene of many a bloody battle, is nowadays devoid of any masonry. All that remains is Fitz-John's earthen mound — not to be dismissed lightly, for this huge motte, surrounded by deep ditches, measures 50 ft from top to bottom.

🚗 *PAINSCASTLE is on the B4594, accessible off the A470 near Erwood south-east of Builth Wells.*

PRESTEIGNE
Powys

When the carriages on the old London to Aberystwyth coaching route decided to stop elsewhere, Presteigne was taken off-the-beaten-track; and there it has remained ever since. Peaceful Presteigne looks out across the River Lugg into England, officially a Welsh settlement — but only just — despite its English-sounding name.

This location is the key to its history. Although nowadays no more than a village, Presteigne was once an important borderland borough town with a charter granted in c. 1225. Welsh forces destroyed its castle in 1262. The church has stood the test of time well. Mainly late 14th century, it incorporates some Saxon work and contains a beautiful Flemish tapestry, early 16th century, depicting the Entry into Jerusalem.

The coaches, when they called, used to stop off at the Radnorshire Arms, a distinguished hostelry dating from 1616 and built in the typical black-and-white half-timbered borderland style.

🚗 *PRESTEIGNE, which straddles the junction of the B4362 and B4355, is about 21 miles east of Llandrindod Wells.*

69

WELSHPOOL
Powys

Powis Castle, on the southern fringes of the town, captures the limelight here. From relatively common beginnings as a borderland castle, Powis progressed through the ranks to end up as a stately home *par excellence*.

Continuous occupation over the centuries saw its metamorphosis from military stronghold to Elizabethan manor to 19th-century country home. Powis's mellow red limestone stonework reveals its ancestry in the surviving medieval Great Gatehouse and keep. A sumptuous interior also spans the centuries, containing medieval weaponry, an Elizabethan Long Gallery and 1688 gilded State Bedchamber of theatrical proportions.

The gardens, The castle crowns a staircase of four grand terraces, a masterpiece of Italianate design. Created between 1688 and 1722, they are horticulturally and historically important as the only formal gardens of this date which survive in their original form. Powis, a National Trust property, also contains the famous Gold Cup woods, one of Britain's finest old oakwoods.

Welshpool is a prosperous market town and long-established hub of communications. The partially restored Welshpool Canal follows the Severn's broad vale, whilst the narrow-gauge Welshpool and Llanfair Light Railway travels westwards for eight miles through pastoral hill country to Llanfair Caereinion. The town is also noteworthy for its half-timbered and Georgian architecture.

🚗 WELSHPOOL, *at the junction of the A483, A458 and A490, lies between Newtown and Shrewsbury.*

Sumptuous Powis Castle

Offa's Dyke

Offa's Dyke charts a roller-coaster route over undulating country

Speculation surrounds the true purpose behind the construction of *Clawdd Offa*, Offa's Dyke, the first official barrier between Wales and England. It is tempting to look upon it as a military border pure and simple, built to keep the troublesome Welsh within their hill country to the west. Yet it is hardly a serious line of defence, in comparison, for example, to the heavily fortified Hadrian's Wall.

All that can be stated with certainty is that it was constructed in the 8th century at the command of King Offa (757-796), ruler of the Midland Kingdom of Mercia. His great earthen barrier, around 20 ft high with a deep ditch on the Welsh side, ran from north to south, separating Saxon from Celt. Offa's precise motives in undertaking such a monumental task are still obscure, though his dyke did unarguably establish the first demarcation line between Wales and England.

Perhaps it was intended more as an administrative than a military border, a marker line which, once and for all, settled squabbles over disputed territory. By the 10th century it had certainly been accepted as the legitimate border, judging by this piece of Saxon law: 'Neither shall a Welshman cross into English land nor an Englishman cross into Welsh land without the appointed man from that other land who should meet him at the bank and bring him back there again without any offence being committed.' Whether this novel system of chaperoning ever caught on properly is not known.

A quick glance at any map of the border country reveals conclusive evidence of the dyke's effectiveness. To the west, Welsh placenames beginning in 'Llan' or 'Tre' abound. Across the dyke, only a few miles to the east, the English suffixes 'ton' and 'ham' are plentiful.

This 1200-year-old earthworks has long since disappeared in parts. In others, it stands miraculously well preserved almost to its original height. Some of its best stretches traverse the remote hills around Knighton. *Clawdd Offa* drives through this quiet countryside just like a miniature railway cutting, its ditch and high banking an atmospheric reminder that this peaceful landscape was, to our remote ancestors, troubled frontier country.

The present border between Wales and England bears only a rough approximation to the dyke, though the Offa's Dyke path deviates as little as possible from the original. This, the most varied of Britain's long-distance footpaths, takes in everything from pastoral lowlands to high moor in its 170-mile route from Prestatyn in the north to the Severn estuary near Chepstow.

Snowdonia

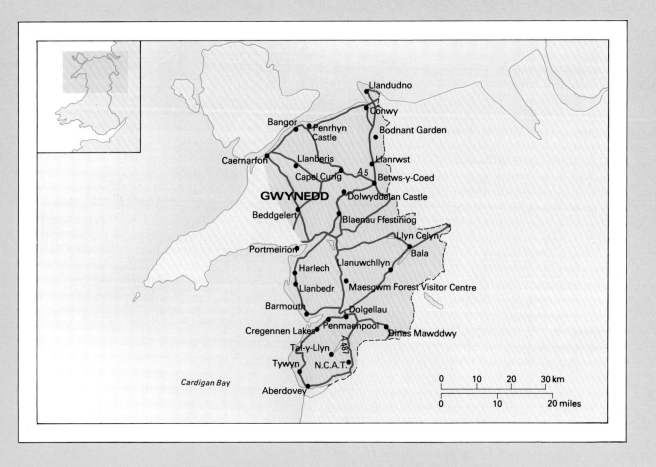

Sunrise from the
summit of Snowdon:
this is the sight
that poet William
Wordsworth aimed for
in his dawn ascent
of the peak, the
highest in England
and Wales

Map labels: Llandudno · Conwy · Bangor · Penrhyn Castle · Bodnant Garden · Caernarfon · Llanberis · Llanrwst · A5 · Capel Curig · Betws-y-Coed · **GWYNEDD** · Dolwyddelan Castle · Beddgelert · Blaenau Ffestiniog · Portmeirion · Llyn Celyn · Bala · Llanuwchllyn · Harlech · Maesgwm Forest Visitor Centre · Llanbedr · Barmouth · Dolgellau · Cregennen Lakes · Penmaenpool · Dinas Mawddwy · Tal-y-Llyn · A487 · Tywyn · N.C.A.T. · Cardigan Bay · Aberdovey · 0 10 20 30 km · 0 10 20 miles

WALES, THE LAND OF mountains, reaches its high point here. And Wales, the land of castles, keeps its most powerful for Snowdonia. North Wales's mountains and medieval fortresses are interlinked, for together they help define Welsh history.

Snowdon, at 3560 ft, stands head and shoulders above everything else. This summit gives its name to the Snowdonia National Park — and in doing so creates a degree of confusion. Snowdonia, at 835 square miles the second largest national park in Britain, extends way beyond Snowdon itself down into Mid Wales. The jagged black-and-purple peaks of Mount Snowdon and its neighbours, white-veined with quartz and born in a volcanic turmoil countless thousands of years ago, preside in the north-west corner of the park. This upland terrain culminates at Cader Idris, the mountain which guards the park's southern gateway.

Historically, this part of Wales was a fountainhead of Welsh aspirations. This was once the ancient kingdom of Gwynedd, home of the native Welsh princes. And it was into this mountain fastness that the Welsh retreated after the 13th-century invasion of Wales. Snowdonia is a dramatic stage on which the backdrops are almost overstated, the historic scenario almost too theatrical. Its steely skies and rocky peaks are, in this sense, a perfect accompaniment to the string of mighty castles which testify both to English ambition and Welsh resistance in those troubled bygone times.

ABERDOVEY
Gwynedd

Aberdovey makes the most of the thin strip of land that lies between the steep green hillsides and the sea at the mouth of the Dyfi estuary. Colourfully painted inns and houses run along the front of this classy little seaside resort, also popular with the golfing fraternity due to its excellent 18-hole course.

Aberdovey's salty prospect amidst the inviting sailing waters of Cardigan Bay has also encouraged its role as a popular water sports centre, a natural evolution from the times, a century or so ago, when its quayside was busy with trading schooners. The sea has also contributed to the well-known 'Bells of Aberdovey', composed by Dibdin for the opera *Liberty Hall*. This familiar song is based on the legend of the drowning of *Cantref-y-Gwaelod* ('the Lowland Hundred'), an area of land now submerged beneath the waters of Cardigan Bay.

Directly north of Aberdovey, a scenic little road travels through a pretty mountain vale — unhappily christened 'Happy Valley' by the Victorians, an ugly label that has unfortunately stuck — which contains the isolated tarn of Llyn Barfog (Bearded Lake).

🚗 *ABERDOVEY is on the A493 coast road, 10 miles south-west of Machynlleth and 4 miles south of Tywyn.*

BALA
Gwynedd

The deep fault between the Aran and Arennig Mountains is partially filled by the waters of four-mile-long Llyn Tegid (Bala Lake), the largest natural lake in Wales. Llyn Tegid has an unique occupant: the gwyniad, a white trout, only to be found here, which keeps itself to itself in the deep waters of the lake.

A scenic narrow-guage railway runs along the lakeside from Llanuwchllyn (see separate entry) to Bala. Bala itself is a thoroughly Welsh, and Welsh-speaking, town — and has been for centuries. The celebrated Welsh Nonconformist, Rev. Thomas Charles (1755-1814), preached here. His statue can be seen outside Capel Tegid, Bala's Presbyterian chapel.

One end of the town's long, tree-lined main street is dominated by another figure in a far less humble pose than that of the Bible-bearing Charles. This is the suitably defiant statue of Thomas Edward Ellis, the 19th-century Liberal M.P who advocated home rule for Wales. The rooftops and chimneys behind almost hide the outline of a strange, tall earthen tump, the remains of a Norman fortification known as Tomen-y-Bala.

🚗 *BALA, at the junction of the A494, A4212 and B4391, is 18 miles north-east of Dolgellau.*

BANGOR
Gwynedd

Visitors will not be tempted to tarry long in this large town at the north-eastern end of the Menai Strait. Historically, it is mainly notable as an early centre of Celtic Christianity. Bangor Cathedral was founded c. A.D. 548 by St Deiniol. Although significant as one of the oldest monastic sites in Britain, it is not in the league of great cathedrals, comparing with St David's only in its siting, close to the sea but sheltered by hills. Between 1866 and 1870, the cathedral saw wholesale restoration, though it retains its historic 13th to 16th-century core.

Modern Bangor is a busy university town and — with the Menai and Britannia Bridges so close by — gateway point for the Isle of Anglesey. The town's Museum of Welsh Antiquities boasts a fine collection of prehistoric and Romano-British finds, medieval artefacts, ceramics, old maps and prints.

🚗 *BANGOR, at the junction of the A5 and A4087, is 9 miles north-east of Caernarfon.*

BARMOUTH
Gwynedd

Barmouth's most flattering face is a distant one. On the road down from the Cregennen Lakes (see separate entry), the resort looks like a child's model, a cluster of grey building blocks arranged neatly around the sands below towering mountain slopes at the mouth of the Mawddach estuary.

Take the train or footpath across the beautiful Mawddach estuary

Close-up acquaintance is something of an anti-climax, for Barmouth's confined streets are cluttered with the bric-à-brac of the seaside trade. On the plus side, the resort has a cheerful character, a most attractive old harbourside and, right on the doorstep of magnificent mountain and coastal scenery, must be one of the best sited in Wales.

National Trust buffs will already know as much, for the view from the Trust's cliffland perch of Dinas Oleu is an all-encompassing one, looking out as it does across the estuary to the mountains of Cader Idris. Not only that: this four-and-a-half-acre site will be dear to their hearts as the first property ever to be acquired by the Trust, in 1895.

There are more fine views from the nearby Panorama Walk and an unusual opportunity to see the waters of the Mawddach (William Wordsworth's 'sublime estuary' which might 'compare with the finest in Scotland') at close quarters by following the walkway that accompanies British Rail's bridge across the mouth of the estuary.

🚗 *BARMOUTH, on the A496, is 10 miles west of Dolgellau and 10 miles south of Harlech.*

BEDDGELERT
Gwynedd

Of all the villages in Snowdonia, this one is a personal favourite. Forget the ridiculous story about Gelert, the faithful hound killed in error by his master and buried in a nearby field — the invention of an enterprising 18th-century hotelier — and concentrate instead on Beddgelert's much-praised natural beauty.

Although only seven miles from the sea, stone-built Beddgelert seems to offer no escape from the mountains. It stands at the confluence of

A bird's eye view of the Nant Gwynant valley, near Beddgelert

the Glaslyn and Colwyn Rivers, surrounded by the towering shoulders of Snowdonia where great slabs of exposed rock begin to break through the thin topsoil.

Wordsworth set off on a dawn ascent of Snowdon from here, an episode he later recalled, in inimitable style, within *The Prelude*. Considering such celebrated publicity, and the village's long standing popularity, Beddgelert remains amazingly unspoilt and uncommercialized.

The Nant Gwynant valley slices through the mountains to the northeast, its narrow floor flooded by two idyllic lakes, Llyn Dinas and Llyn Gwynant. The most famous local beauty spot, though, is to be found directly south of the village where the Glaslyn forces a passage through a rocky defile known as the Aberglasyn Pass, its 700-ft-high cliffs and narrow dimensions making sure that the sun rarely penetrates as far as the wooded riverbanks. It comes as something of a surprise to learn that, not so long ago, when the river was tidal, ships were able to sail right up to the picturesque stone bridge at the southern approach to the pass.

🚗 *BEDDGELERT, at the junction of the A4085 and A498, is 13 miles south-east of Caernarfon.*

BETWS-Y-COED
Gwynedd

Inland beauty spots do not come much more famous than this one. Ever since the early 19th century, coaches, trains — and now cars — have deposited visitors at this spot in the wooded foothills of Snowdonia. Yet one cannot help but register a faint tinge of disappointment, for there are certainly prettier and more peaceful places to be found amongst the hills and mountains of North Wales.

Betws-y-coed's charm lies more in its surroundings than the town itself, a long, grey-stoned line of hotels, guesthouses and shops with no identifiable centre. The town stands in a wooded glen where the bare, elemental shoulders of the Snowdon massif have declined into more civilized hill country, dotted with tarns and lakes (Llyn Geirionydd, to the north, is delightful) and criss-crossed by innumerable forest trails.

Betws-y-coed is also close to the meeting place of three rivers, the Conwy, Llugwy and Lledr — which explains this area's plethora of waterfalls. Best known of all, of course, are the Swallow Falls just over a mile west of the town where the Llugwy cascades over great rocks in a wooded gorge. Less famous, but more spectacular, are the Conwy Falls located in the hills a few miles to the east of Betws-y-coed.

Swallow Falls is near the rightly-named Ugly House, a small cottage beside the road made from huge, ill-fitting boulders and looking like something out of a child's nightmare. The old bridge of Pont-y-Pair, in the town itself, is a much more accomplished example of the stonemason's art though it cannot rival the nearby Waterloo Bridge, an ornate iron construction designed by Thomas Telford and erected at the end of the Napoleonic Wars in 1815. True to the spirit of regional equality, it is splendidly decorated with motifs depicting roses, thistles, shamrocks and leeks.

BETWS-Y-COED, at the junction of the A5 and A470, is 20 miles south of Llandudno, 10 miles northeast of Blaenau Ffestiniog.

Telford's Waterloo Bridge at Betwys-y-coed, built in the days before bridges became boring

BLAENAU FFESTINIOG
Gwynedd

Twenty-five years ago, Blaenau Ffestiniog, the former 'slate capital of the world', was a has-been. Its star had ascended and burned brightly in the late 19th century, when thousands of men worked by candlelight in the labyrinthine slate chambers hewn into its mountainsides, producing roofing material for a house-hungry world.

In decline, this tightly packed, terraced town was perceived as the black hole in the middle of Snowdonia. Thanks to the unquenchable inquisitiveness of the modern tourist and the enterprise of a few locals, Blaenau Ffestiniog's star is now on the ascendant again. The town's narrow streets are choked with summer visitors, and a qualified gaeity (North Waleans are not famous for their unbridled sense of fun) has replaced the gloom.

The reasons behind Blaenau Ffestiniog's new lease of life are certainly two, and possibly four-fold. The pyramidal piles of debris and jagged screes of discarded slate waste in the hills around the town mark the sites of two mines, first opened to the public in the early 1970s. Around 200,000 visitors now come to the Llechwedd Slate Caverns each year, to ride by electric tramway through its old chambers or to take the 'Deep Mine' tour. Similar numbers turn up at the rival Gloddfa Ganol Mountain Centre opposite, advertised as 'the largest slate mine in the world'. No one can dispute the size of this vast site, with its underground passageways, exhibitions and working slate mill, which seems to take up the entire mountainside.

The Ffestiniog Railway (see Porthmadog entry) provides the third reason for Blaenau Ffestiniog's renaissance. After years of dedicated work by enthusiasts, this narrow-gauge line now runs again all the way from Porthmadog to Blaenau Ffestiniog, with passengers replacing its original cargoes of slate. The Stwlan Dam, 1000 ft high in the mountains above the town and part of an imaginative hydro-electricity scheme, also attracts visitors — especially since it is possible to drive or take a bus right up to its lofty lakeside.

BLAENAU FFESTINIOG is at the junction of the A470 and A496, 21 miles north of Dolgellau.

BODNANT GARDEN
Gwynedd

The Welsh are not noted for their green fingers. Perhaps it is a case of quality rather than quantity, for the formal gardens at Bodnant — a rare feature in Wales — are amongst Britain's finest.

This 97-acre garden, a National Trust property, has the advantage of a superb location in the Vale of Conwy, along the gentle, pastoral eastern fringe of Snowdonia. The product of three centuries of careful development and grooming, Bodnant is an harmonious blend of natural and decorative influences.

There are fountains and exuberant ballustrading here, complementing a profusion of flowering shrubs and plants. Camelias, azaleas, magnolias and roses grow in colourful abundance, though the outstanding spectacle for many comes in the early summer, when Bodnant's rhododendrons are in full bloom. The garden terraces, part of Bodnant's outstanding landscape modelling — which also include a formal lily pond — command marvellous views across the valley to Snowdonia.

BODNANT GARDEN is accessible off the A470, 8 miles south of Llandudno.

CAERNARFON
Gwynedd

Those unaware of the sensitivities of Welsh history are invariably surprised to discover that not all Welshmen are particularly enamoured of Caernarfon Castle. This imperious medieval fortress, quite easily the best known of all the Welsh castles, strikes an ambivalent chord within Wales. Understand Caernarfon, and you begin to comprehend the complexities of the Welsh character.

Imperious Caernarfon, undimmed by night. Edward I would have appreciated such flattering floodlights

Begun in 1283, Caernarfon put the final stamp of authority on the conquest of North Wales by the English king, Edward I. The castle was designed to serve as more than a mere fortress. This was the palace and official government residence of the English monarch and his successors.

Caernarfon is still almost all that it originally set out to be. Alteration, repair and extensive restoration from the Victorian period onward have not erased its character, a composite of military strength and regal authority. None of Edward's other Welsh castles, for example, boasts Caernarfon's decorative bands of coloured stone, a feature which has been compared to the walls of Constantinople.

The castle's polygonal towers are also exceptional, especially the Eagle Tower, crowned by three tall, slender turrets. With so much in the way of magnificence, it is difficult to single out other architectural features, though the King's and Queen's Gates — the former still serving as the main entrance — are particularly fine.

It was from the ramparts of this palace-castle that, according to legend anyway, Edward is said to have presented his baby son to the Welsh as 'the native-born prince who could speak no English' (sober historians are inclined to think that the venue was Rhuddlan, if it took place at all). Within modern times, the castle has been used for the investitures of the Princes of Wales, the most recent of which was 1969 when Prince Charles was invested.

The foundations of another, earlier stronghold in Caernarfon are overshadowed by the presence of the castle. This is *Segontium*, a Roman fort built on the hill above the town, and dating from around A.D. 78.

◄ *CAERNARFON, at the junction of the A487, A4085 and A4086 is 9 miles south-west of Bangor.*

CAPEL CURIG
Gwynedd

The highest peaks in England and Wales surround this mountain village. The Snowdonia massif has 13 main summits dominated, of course, by 3560-ft-high Snowdon itself, the highest peak in Britain south of the Scottish Highlands and known in Welsh as *Eryri* ('The abode of the eagle').

Its jagged profile and razor-sharp ridges can be seen emerging out of the cloud and mist from the Pen-y-Pass area at the head of the Llanberis Pass, four miles south-west of Capel Curig. The isolated Pen-y-Gwryd Hotel here is now part of mountaineering folklore. This inn was the original base camp for the first successful attempt on Everest in 1953, the team training in these mountains prior to setting off for the Himalayas — and leaving their names on Pen-y-Gwryd's ceiling to prove it.

Tryfan was their tough testing ground. This 3010-ft mountain is part of the Carneddau, a collective name for Wales's second highest mountain range. Soaring up from the roadside as one towering, unbroken block of exposed rock, Tryfan is just as challenging as neighbouring Snowdon.

The gouging, destructive effects of glaciation are everywhere to be seen in this primeval, boulder-strewn landscape. Huge sheets of ice were responsible for the steep slopes, cwms and mountain lakes around the Nant Ffrancon Pass to the north-west of Capel Curig. Really serious walkers, for whom Snowdon itself is a little *passé*, reckon that North Wales's raw, elemental personality is nowhere stronger than it is here, amongst the peaks of Carnedd Dafydd (3424 ft) and Carnedd Llywelyn (3485 ft), the latter named after the long-lamented Welsh prince who met his death in 1282 fighting the English.

◄ *CAPEL CURIG is at the junction of the A5 and A4086, 15 miles southeast of Bangor and 5 miles west of Betws-y-coed.*

CONWY
Gwynedd

Photographers in search of the ultimate medieval castle-cum-mountain shot invariably end up in Conwy. If they are adept enough, they capture even more, for Conwy Castle in its Snowdonia setting is only part of the picture.

Conwy is all about mood and atmosphere — an authentic medieval atmosphere, stronger here than in any other town in Wales. Mighty Caernarfon, Wales's most famous castle, comes a poor second to Conwy in this respect. Well scrubbed and immaculately renovated Caernarfon is not as convincing in its ability to recreate the medieval spirit which pervades the rough, tough, grey-green walls of Conwy.

Comparisons are perhaps unfair, for Conwy's character is aided and abetted by a ring of medieval town walls which are amongst the finest and most complete in Europe. Conwy the military stronghold and Conwy the garrison town are almost as well integrated today as they were at their conception, 800 years ago. The town walls, protected by no less than 22 towers, run for over three-quarters of a mile amongst narrow streets that spill down to the pretty, boat-filled quayside.

The original street plan survives — as do some of the houses. Three-storeyed Aberconwy House (National Trust) dates from the 14th century and is one of the last remaining timber-framed buildings in the town.

Plas Mawr is an imposing 16th-century town house famous for its inventive, ornamental plasterwork. A little light relief is provided by the tiny dwelling on the quayside, reputedly the smallest house in Britain and furnished as a Welsh cottage.

Every house in Conwy, whatever its size, is well and truly dwarfed by the castle, a masterpiece of late 13th-century military architecture which makes the most of a confined promontory above the strategic Deganwy estuary where the River Conwy meets the sea. Eight massive round towers and soaring curtain walls tell us, better than any text book, that this was a castle built by Edward I to strike fear into the hearts of the Welsh.

Conwy's cornucopia of architectural heritage goes on and on. The footbridge which spans the estuary is not quite as old as it looks. Put up in the 1820s and the work of Thomas Telford, its mock-military appearance was designed to match the castle. Robert Stephenson's tubular railway bridge, also castellated, was built alongside in 1848. In the late 1950s, all motor traffic was transferred from Telford's sympathetic structure to a modern bridge — devoid, of course, of any such 19th-century niceties — based on an inappropriately functional design.

◄ *CONWY is on the A55 near Llandudno Junction, 15 miles northeast of Bangor, 4 miles south of Llandudno.*

Thomas Telford's 19th-century approach bridge, built in castellated style, in no way compromises the authentic medieval atmosphere of Conwy's towers and curtain walls. Conwy may not be Wales's greatest castle, but measured by its force of personality, it stands unchallenged

CREGENNEN LAKES
Gwynedd

This pair of lakes are hidden away above the luxuriant Mawddach estuary on the northern slopes of Cader Idris. Their most direct approach, up a narrow, hairpinned road that climbs with alacrity the 1000 ft to Cregennen from sea-level at Arthog, is almost as memorable as the lakes themselves.

In its lower reaches, the road winds upwards along a thickly wooded valley before breaking out onto the bare, exposed shoulders of Cader Idris. The lakes lie in glorious open countryside, Cader's north-facing escarpment sweeping down to their waters. Largely unknown and unvisited 15 years ago, Cregennen Lakes are now becoming an increasingly well-trodden beauty spot. In the care of the National Trust, they remain thankfully devoid of any commercial development.

Motorists wary of the direct ascent can take an easier approach road. They should, though, summon up the will to follow the road back down to Arthog (the descent is always easier) for the panoramic views en route of the swirling waters, sands and woodlands along the lovely Mawddach estuary and the resort of Barmouth, perched at its entrance.

🚗 *CREGENNEN LAKES can be approached by minor road off the A493 at Arthog, 5 miles south-west of Dolgellau; alternatively, by an easier minor road running directly to the lakes from Dolgellau.*

DINAS MAWDDWY
Gwynedd

This little village nestles, Swiss-fashion, amongst steep, pine-clad slopes in the high, mountainous upper reaches of the Dyfi Valley. The Meirion Woollen Mill, on the outskirts, still looks like what it once was: the village's railway station, the end of the line for trains travelling from Machynlleth.

The last train ran in 1951. Disused station site then became woollen mill which, after a few false starts, prospered from the late Sixties onwards. The Meirion Woollen Mill is now firmly on the map as one of the best known in Wales. Visitors are welcomed into its workshops, where the noisy weaving frames produce the colourfully patterned cloths and tapestries distinctive to Wales. As an extra attraction, the mill has converted the original railway station house into a café rightly renowned for its traditional Welsh teas. Stop off here — as the regulars do — if you are making the north-south journey through Wales on the A470 trunk route.

Pont Minllyn, near the mill, is a picturesque early 17th-century bridge across the Dyfi. The Brigand's Inn at Mallwyd, a little further south, is named after the *Gwylliaid Cochion Mawddwy* ('the wild red brigands of Mawddwy'), red-haired robbers who terrorised this area in the 16th century.

🚗 *DINAS MAWDDWY is on the A470, 9 miles east of Dolgellau.*

DOLGELLAU
Gwynedd

Visitors either love or loathe Dolgellau. Some find its uniformity of character oppressive, built as it is almost entirely of huge blocks of dark local stone which assume a weighty depth of blackness on not-infrequent drizzly days. With no respite from the town's dark slate roofs, Dolgellau is not a place for depressives on a wet Welsh Sunday. Others, in all fairness, are enchanted by the sombre dignity

Dolgellau's classic setting, beneath hill, forest and mountain

of the place, its sense of presence, solidity and robustness of architecture, tall buildings, narrow alleyways and shady nooks and crannies.

Cader Idris is another element in the love-hate equation. This boulder-strewn mountain — lower than Snowdon by 600 ft but no less challenging — looms menacingly above the rooftops. Again, some can live quite happily with this misty, omnipresent Sword of Damocles above their heads. Others find its presence disturbing, their reactions echoing the local legend that those who spend a night on the summit of 'The Chair of Idris' (hence its Welsh name) will awake a poet or madman — or not at all.

Make your own mind up about Dolgellau. On the positive side, it is undisputedly one of the best-located centres from which to tour the Snowdonia National Park. Fans of the town will be pleased to hear that it has now acquired a by-pass, freeing its attractive/gloomy town square from traffic congestion.
🚗 *DOLGELLAU is at the junction of the A470, A493 and A494, 13 miles north of Machynlleth.*

DOLWYDDELAN CASTLE
Gwynedd

This is the real thing. In complete contrast to the Caernarfons and Conwys of this world, castles built by the invading English in the 13th century, Dolwyddelan is a rare surviving example of a fortress put up by the native Welsh.

This proud little castle, of characteristic single tower construction, still stands its ground amongst the rugged mountain country it once commanded. Dolwyddelan dates from the early 13th century, and was probably built by Llywelyn the Great, 'Lord of Snowdon'.

Mighty Harlech, one of the 'top four' of the hundreds of Welsh castles

Llywelyn's castle would have guarded the mountain pass now traversed by the modern road that runs beneath the defences. This strategic consideration, accompanied by some wonderful views, can be appreciated by climbing to the top of the battlements.
🚗 *DOLWYDDELAN is on the A470 mid-way between Blaenau Ffestiniog and Betws-y-coed.*

HARLECH
Gwynedd

Only a handful of the hundreds of castles in Wales are anything approaching household names. Harlech Castle is one of them. This may partly be due to the song *Men of Harlech*, a stirring march inspired by a stout defence of the castle during the Wars of the Roses. Harlech's true celebrity value, though, is a consequence of its stonework and siting.

Academics not noted for their capacity to express natural enthusiasm have been known to rhapsodise over this insolent, grey-stoned fortress, likening it to the military equivalent of a great Gothic cathedral. It was built between 1283 and 1289 and, even today, 700 years on, expresses its original intentions plainly and unequivocally.

This was a castle, one of the so-called 'iron ring' which included Caernarfon and Conwy, built by the English king, Edward I, to contain the native Welsh in their mountain fastness. Harlech's massive twin-towered gatehouse, walls and towers, stand almost to their original height, their stature enhanced by the clever siting of the castle on the summit of a precipitous crag.

From the lofty wall walks, sweeping views encompass not only the distant peaks of Snowdonia into which the Welsh retreated, but also the waters of Tremadog Bay and the long arm of the Lleyn Peninsula. When Harlech was constructed, the sea lapped at its feet. Over the centuries, the sea has receded by over half-a-mile beyond the dunes and sands of Morfa Harlech, leaving the castle high and dry on its landlocked crag. Harlech's 'Way from the Sea', a rocky stairway cut into the cliff, now leads from the castle down to the town's railway station.

Harlech's history reveals an interesting irony which would not have been appreciated by its builder. Constructed by an English king intent on the conquest of Wales, the castle was captured in 1404 by the native leader Owain Glyndwr, who then proceeded to hold a Welsh parliament here.
🚗 *HARLECH, on the A496, is located between Barmouth and Penrhyndeudraeth.*

A Land of Castles

The only Welsh cliché that happens to be true is the one that labels the country 'a land of castles'. No one is quite sure of the precise number here, though experts are happy to quote figures in excess of 400, giving Wales one of the highest concentrations of fortified sites in the world.

This figure encompasses over 1000 years of Welsh history, starting with the first rough-and-ready earth-and-timber defences thrown up hastily by the Normans and ending with the opulent 'sham' castles and follies constructed by *nouveaux riches* 19th-century industrialists. Forget the text books. There is no better way to get to grips with the complexities and contradictions of Wales's tortuous past than through its castles, over 100 of which are open to visitors.

The strongholds built by the Norman invaders had to be both cheap and easy to put up: hence the rash of crude motte-and-bailey castles that appeared throughout Wales from the 11th century. The motte, an earthen mound, overlooked a bailey, or enclosure, the entire site protected by timber defences and ditches.

Remnants of these rudimentary castles are scattered everywhere. Some appear as strangely-shaped tumps, marooned amongst farmers' fields. Others were subsequently strengthened or rebuilt as stone gradually began to replace timber. The coming of these stronger, second-generation sites dates from the construction at Chepstow in c.1070 of Wales's — and Britain's — first stone-built castle.

Medieval fortresses reached a peak of power and sophistication in the great ring of castles built by the English king, Edward I, in his late 13th-century campaigns against Wales. Caernarfon, Conwy, Harlech and Beaumaris are today cited as being amongst the most outstanding examples of medieval military architecture surviving in Europe.

In complete contrast to the mighty Edwardian castles, those built by the native Welsh were much simpler, often single tower affairs (Dolwyddelan in Snowdonia is a classic example), never intended to dominate by force of arms. In the more settled later Middle Ages, castles in Wales became more decorative, less defensive, developing domestic features such as mullioned windows and fine apartments.

From here, it was a short step to the stately home: Chirk Castle, a sumptuously appointed country mansion, is the perfect example, having started life as a medieval fort. The 19th century added the final touch, when mock-medieval and Neo-Norman 'castles' made their appearance, redolent of the wealth and lordly pretensions generated by the Industrial Revolution.

Handsome Raglan marked the end of an era in castle building

LLANBEDR
Gwynedd

The village of Llanbedr stands just inland from a curious stretch of Cardigan Bay coastline known as Mochras. Its alternative name of Shell Island is misleading on one count: the 'island' is a long, narrowing peninsula of sand dunes and peaceful beaches, though the shells are plentiful enough, with over 200 varieties recorded here.

Another curiosity lies landwards of Llanbedr. These are the so-called 'Roman Steps', a well engineered pathway of hundreds of stone steps leading up into the Rhinog Mountains from the remote, romantic lake of Llyn Cwm Bychan. A minor road winds its way up the Artro Valley north-east of the village, ending just past the lakeside. A footpath then takes advantage of the ready-made stone staircase — probably medieval but certainly not Roman in origin — as it climbs into the Rhinogs. These mountains, a shapeless, inhospitable upland mass of exposed rock and heather moor, rise to just under 2500 ft. Few who have tramped this arduous, totally empty terrain will argue with its inclusion amongst Britain's last true wilderness areas, especially in winter.

At Llanfair, just north of Llanbedr, visitors can don miners' helmets for a guided tour of the Old Llanfair Slate Caverns. *Muriau'r Gwyddelod* ('Irishmen's Walls') between Llanfair and Harlech are Iron Age hut circles with well preserved walls four feet high and 18 ft thick in places.

LLANBEDR is on the A496, 3 miles south of Harlech.

An exciting toll road, cut into the cliffside, clings to the Great Orme Headland, Llandudno

LLANDUDNO
Gwynedd

Here we have the regal doyen, the self-appointed but unchallenged 'Queen of the Welsh resorts'. Llandudno is a seaside town redolent of great charm and style. The resort stands aloof from the rest, distanced in character if not geography from its nearby North Wales neighbours and retaining an olde worlde charm.

Like Tenby in the south, Llandudno has not succumbed to the garish excesses that blight so many of Britain's seaside resorts. In Llandudno's case, this is especially commendable, for it has had to deal with the pressures — and put aside the temptations — that come with having the largest selection of hotels in Wales.

Very little has been allowed to compromise its Victorian and Edwardian ambience (in fact, Llandudno is now becoming recognised as one of the most outstanding and best preserved Victorian towns in Britain). Its promenade is particularly splendid. A long row of tall, gabled hotels, painted in muted, pastel tones, stretches into the distance following the gentle curve of the North Beach.

The entire scene is framed between two natural features — the headlands of the Great and Little Ormes. The 679-ft-high Great Orme can be ascended, alpine-style, by cabinlift or on a San Franciscan mode of transport, a cable car tramway. A spectacular coastal toll road has also been cut into its vertical cliffs beneath the tiny headland Church of St Tudno, Llandudno's original place of worship.

This church is much older than the town below, for Llandudno is largely a by-product of the latter part of the 19th century. It represents a coastal equivalent to the inland resort of Llandrindod Wells (see separate entry) as a purpose-built holiday centre. Both share the same uniformity of style, though in Llandudno's case even the street plans are rigidly controlled, conforming to a grid-iron pattern reminiscent of an American town or city. The rule is relaxed only along the pretty shopping centre adorned with decorative iron-and-glass canopies, the streets of which curve in a carefully contrived arc.

Llandudno's North Beach is its busiest, sweeping along the shore from the ornate pier — a prized feature which completes the picture of a Victorian seaside resort in aspic. Along Llandudno's second beach, the West Shore, stands the White Rabbit memorial which commemorates the resort's associations with Charles Dodgson, alias Lewis Carroll, author of *Alice in Wonderland*.

LLANDUDNO is on the A546 between Colwyn Bay and Conwy.

LLANBERIS
Gwynedd

Llanberis stands beside its twin lakes, Llyn Padarn and Peris, at the foot of the Llanberis Pass. This deep cleft, the most famous mountain pass in Snowdonia, was put on the map in the 1950s through the exploits of such pioneering rock climbers as Joe Brown and the late Don Whillans. With little more in the way of equipment than plimsolls and a length of borrowed clothes line, they conquered the fearsome rock slabs and shuddering overhangs that fill this baleful valley.

The little town, at the foot of the highest mountain in England and Wales, has developed into a busy tourist centre. Many are attracted by the Snowdon Mountain Railway, the lazy man's way to reach the top of Snowdon. Weather permitting, the railway's specially designed rack-and-pinion Swiss locomotives climb the four-and-a-half miles from Llanberis to the 3560-ft summit.

Llanberis's second narrow-gauge line — the Llanberis Lake Railway — is pretty enough, though suffers from comparison to its tough big brother. This little line runs along the north-eastern shore of Llyn Padarn for two miles from a terminus near a museum which introduces visitors to a 19th-century industry which dominated these parts. Llanberis's Welsh Slate Museum has a head start in the authenticity stakes for the museum consists of the former workshops of the Dinorwic Quarry. Much of the original machinery has been preserved intact, including a giant water-wheel, over 50 ft in diameter.

Man continues to hew and dig

The twin lakes at the foot of the famous Llanberis Pass

84

amongst these mountains. Although there is now little external evidence of it, the slopes opposite Llanberis are riddled with giant tunnels and man-made caverns, part of the largest pumped storage hydro-electric scheme in Europe. The Central Electricity Generating Board have joined with the National Museum of Wales in creating *Oriel Eryri* ('The Snowdon Gallery'), an interpretive centre which concentrates on the local environment.

Dolbadarn Castle, on a headland where the two lakes meet, is a single tower fortress, built to a typical design by the Welsh leader Llywelyn the Great in the early 13th century.

🚗 *LLANBERIS is on the A4086, 8 miles south-east of Caernarfon.*

LLANRWST
Gwynedd

This pretty little market town assumes the role of 'capital of the Conwy Valley'. Its delicate, three-arched stone bridge over the river is more robust than it looks. Inigo Jones's most famous Welsh work, it dates from 1636.

At the far end is the 15th-century National Trust property, Tu Hwnt i'r Bont, its location plain to any Welsh-speaker for its name means 'At the other side of the bridge'. The building, once a courthouse, was later split into two cottages.

The riverside Gwydir Chapel adjoins St Grwst's Church, just off the main square. The church contains a magnificent rood screen, though the real treasure lies within the 17th-century chapel — an ornately carved stone coffin in which was buried Llywelyn ab Iorwerth, Llywelyn the Great, Wales's much-lauded 13th-century leader.

A series of beautiful, little-visited lakes hide themselves away in the pine-clad hills above Llanrwst (Llyn Geirionydd and Llyn Crafnant are particularly attractive). Seekers of obscure religious sites will also want to visit Gwydir Uchaf Chapel (*uchaf* meaning upper), tucked discreetly away amongst the trees. Built in 1673 as a private chapel, it is notable for its carvings and ceiling paintings.

🚗 *LLANRWST, at the junction of the A470, B5106 and B5427, is 15 miles south of Llandudno.*

LLANUWCHLLYN
Gwynedd

This village has grown up around the south-western end of Bala Lake. It is the terminus of the narrow-gauge Bala Lake Railway, one of the 'Great Little Trains of Wales', which runs along the southern shores of the lake for four-and-a-half miles to the outskirts of Bala.

Llanuwchllyn is also linked to Bala in a cultural sense through shared, deeply felt and continuing associations with the Welsh language. Statues of two famous Welshmen — Sir Owen Morgan Edwards (1858-1920) and Sir Ifan ab Owen Edwards (1895-1970) — stand here. Sir Owen, born on a local farm, championed the survival and spread of the Welsh language. The torch was later carried by his son, Sir Ifan, who founded *Urdd Gobaith Cymru* ('the Welsh League of Youth').

Farming traditions live on at the Cyffdy Farm Park at Parc, in the remote foothills of the Arennig Mountains north of Llanuwchllyn. Visitors are welcome to wander through this typical hill sheep farm ranged around a solid, stone-built farmhouse dating from the early 17th century.

🚗 *LLANUWCHLLYN is just off the A494, 14 miles north-east of Dolgellau.*

LLYN CELYN
Gwynedd

This two-mile-long 16,000 million gallon lake was constructed to supply North-east Wales and Cheshire no more than 20 years ago. Surprise at its relative youth is registered because this man-made lake, unlike others in Wales, looks as though it has been here for much longer, a consequence of sympathetic planning and landscaping.

The eye leads naturally from its wide waters to the Arennig Mountains, rising majestically from Llyn Celyn's southern shore. Along its northern shoreline, a starkly simple and modern stone chapel stands as a replacement to the original place of worship, drowned beneath the waters in the flooded valley below. Capel Celyn Memorial was 'designed to resemble a ship coming in from over the water'. Stones from the lost chapel went into its building, and headstones rescued from the now submerged graveyard have been re-erected alongside. Within the chapel, three magnificently carved slate slabs list those whose bodies lie beneath the lake.

Just east of Llyn Celyn's grass-covered dam, the River Tryweryn rushes along a stretch which has become a white-water canoe slalom course of international repute.

🚗 *LLYN CELYN, 5 miles north-west of Bala, is accessible by the A4212.*

MAESGWM FOREST VISITOR CENTRE
Gwynedd

Coed-y-Brenin, a large Forestry Commission plantation north of Dolgellau, holds many secrets. In medieval times, it was an estate of the Welsh princes. Later, it witnessed Wales's 19th-century gold rush. Today, the blanketing effect that conifers bring fails to disguise this area's inherent natural beauty. Copses of ancient oakwoods and other deciduous trees survive amongst the pines. Waterfalls and crystal rivers rush and tumble through Coed-y-Brenin's dense heart. Regimented greenery has, for once, been unable to swamp the natural lie of the land.

The commission's many enemies consider the conifer, *en masse*, an alien, destructive army, a destroyer of landscapes and vistas. In all fairness, the commission is not unaware of these arguments and within the last 15 years or so has made worthy attempts to explain its position, to open up the forests to visitors, and to increase the amenity and recreational value of woodlands such as Coed-y-Brenin.

Maesgwm is a consequence of all this. Interestingly presented displays tell the history of Coed-y-Brenin's 217,000 acres, also introducing the visitor to the network of over 50 miles of waymarked trails that now run through the forest.

The centre also touches on Coed-y-Brenin's most alluring secret: gold. The Dolgellau gold belt, which stretches from the Mawddach estuary into the forest's cool, green heart, attracted a Klondike-like rush of 19th-century prospectors. Gold is still mined here — somewhere. Of the past endeavours, the ruined mine at Gwynfynydd is undoubtedly the most evocative, with the bonus of a beautiful location. Follow the minor road which leads north-east through the trees from Ganllwyd, a village on the A470 just over two miles south of Maesgwm. When the tarmac ends, walk the rest of the way (about a mile) to two lovely waterfalls, Rhaeadr Mawddach and Pistyll-y-Cain, and the shell of Gwynfynydd, a mine which yielded rich pickings in the mid and late 19th century.

🚗 *MAESGWM is just off the A470, 7 miles north of Dolgellau, approximately 19 miles south-east of Porthmadog.*

NATIONAL CENTRE FOR ALTERNATIVE TECHNOLOGY
Gwynedd

In the early Seventies, a group of committed conservationists moved into a derelict, barren slate quarry in the conifer-clad hills north of Machynlleth — an unpromising environment indeed in which to conduct an experiment in self-sufficiency and alternative living. The success of their 'village of the future', which now produces much of its own energy and food, speaks for itself.

This unique site does not exist just for the dedicated conservationist. Anyone with the faintest interest in the creative management of finite energy resources will be fascinated by the work taking place here. Amongst the ingenious array of devices employed — some simple, others of a Heath Robinson-like complexity — there are aerogenerators (windmills to you and me), water-powered turbines, banks of solar panels, woodgas systems, methane gardens and buildings heavily insulated to minimise heat loss.

The centre has also stumbled on an alternative means of income, thanks to an inquisitive tourist market. Open to visitors throughout the year, it is now Wales's most unconventional tourist attraction. Its brochures, of course, are printed on re-cycled paper.

🚗 *N.C.A.T. is signposted off the A487 at Pantperthog, about 3 miles north of Machynlleth and 13 miles south of Dolgellau.*

PENMAENPOOL
Gwynedd

Start your exploration of the Mawddach estuary's southern shores from this quirky little spot, at the end of a rickety toll bridge which crosses from the northern bank. A ghostly railway signal box, signal gantry and faint remnants of platform mark the eastern end of the Morfa Mawddach walk, a five-mile footpath which follows the waterside course laid by the redundant Great Western Region railway line.

The signal box now serves as a Wildlife Information Centre, and is a perfect place from which to observe cormorants, herons and oystercatchers, some of the many species that frequent the waters of the estuary.

Fairbourne, six miles to the southwest, is the home of a narrow-gauge railway — the smallest of the lot in Wales, with a gauge of only 12 and a quarter inches — that runs for two miles along a sandy spit to the mouth of the estuary.

PENMAENPOOL is on the A493, 2 miles west of Dolgellau.

PENRHYN CASTLE
Gwynedd

This gigantic sham castle expresses the exuberant, over-confident, anything-goes spirit of the 19th century perfectly. Built between 1820 and 1837 for local magnate Lord Penrhyn, it is the North Wales equivalent to the south's Cardiff Castle, the Victorian palace that Lord Bute created for himself from the proceeds of the coal trade.

In the north, the slate quarries and a lucrative sugar trading business allowed Lord Penrhyn to indulge his whimsies. He employed architect Thomas Hopper to create for him a cavernous mock castle that is now regarded as the best example in Britain of the Norman revival.

Penrhyn's enormous four-storeyed Neo-Norman keep is just the beginning. Inside as well as out, the architect's zest was evidently unstoppable. Hardly any surface is left unadorned; nearly every excess is indulged. Quite understandably, Queen Victoria is reputed to have refused to sleep in the enormous bed — made of course from slate — which weighs in at over a ton.

Penrhyn Castle, a National Trust property, stands in magnificent 47-acre grounds and also contains a noteworthy doll collection and railway museum.

PENRHYN, on the eastern approach to Bangor, is accessible from an entrance near the junction of the A5 and A55.

PORTMEIRION
Gwynedd

This is easily the most un-Welsh village in Wales. Portmeirion, a creation of the architect and iconoclast Sir Clough Williams-Ellis (who died in 1978, aged 95), throws convention to the wind. Visitors are advised to expect the unexpected at Portmeirion, his bizarre little kingdom in which renaissance Italy rubs shoulders with 18th-century England, where flights of stone steps lead puzzlingly to nowhere in particular, and whose boat, moored to the harbour wall, is a life-sized model in concrete.

The village, created piecemeal over the years by Sir Clough, is an architectural pot-pourri of styles and influences which reflect his 'gay, light-opera sort of approach'. Humour was an essential element in his repertoire. Architectural jokes and unexpected touches appear around almost every corner; elaborate facades flatter only to

The portal into Portmeirion, a magical, other-worldly village

deceive, fronting absolutely nothing, in the way of flimsy film sets on Hollywood back lots.

Portmeirion's other-worldliness is enhanced by its location at the far end of a secluded, densely wooded little peninsula. The village is now forever identified with actor Patrick McGoohan's cult Sixties television series, *The Prisoner*, in which it became the strange, inexplicable prison-domain. Portmeirion's strong sense of displacement — it should by all rights be located in the sunny south of Italy, not in blustery, damp North Wales — was the perfect architectural complement to McGoohan's surreal storyline.

PORTMEIRION is accessible off the A487 at Minffordd, between Porthmadog and Penrhyndeudraeth.

Sheep safely graze beneath Bird Rock on meadows once covered by the seas of Cardigan Bay

TAL-Y-LLYN
Gwynedd

This lovely lake, sheltering beneath the green foothills and rocky scree slopes of Cader Idris, gives its name to a long valley, a major geological fault caused by a crack in the earth's crust. The valley, running from the lake south-westwards towards Tywyn, was first fashioned by a river before being scooped into its present deep and emphatic shape by the action of glaciers during the Ice Age.

The B4405 road follows the line of the valley (as does the Talyllyn Railway — see Tywyn entry). At Abergynolwyn, the River Dysynni takes a sharp turn through a narrow defile into a side valley. This detour away from Tal-y-llyn is also worth following by road, for it reveals a trio of fascinating and largely undiscovered places of interest.

Craig-yr-Aderyn, or Bird Rock, is an ornothological oddity. Before the vale silted up, this craggy precipice was a sea-cliff. No one seems to have

told the cormorants that the ocean is now four miles away, for these seabirds continue to nest here well away from the waters of Cardigan Bay.

Further up the valley stand the atmospheric ruins of Castell-y-Bere, a 'proper' Welsh castle in the sense that this mountain fortress was a stronghold of the Welsh native princes as opposed to the invading English. Probably built in 1221, it served as the court of no less a personage than Llywelyn ab Iorwerth, Llywellyn the Great, Prince of Gwynedd.

A ruin of more modest dimensions lies near the end of the tarmac road at the cul-de-sac hamlet of Llanfihangel-y-pennant. A commemorative stone explains its significance as the remains of Mary Jones's cottage. In 1800, 16-year-old Mary walked from here across the mountains, barefoot for part of the way, to collect a Welsh Bible from the great Methodist

preacher, Rev. Thomas Charles. Her arduous 25-mile journey is said to have inspired the foundation, by Charles, of the British and Foreign Bible Society.

TAL-Y-LLYN valley is accessible from the east at Minffordd on the A487. From the west, approach it off the A493 north-east of Tywyn.

TYWYN
Gwynedd

Tywyn is a rather forlorn seaside town which time and fashion seem to have passed by. Today's visitors do better to treat it as a well located touring centre rather than a resort, for Tywyn's hinterland is made up of the spectacular Cader Idris massif.

The Talyllyn Narrow Gauge Railway, one of the 'Great Little Trains of Wales', chuffs inland from Tywyn to a remote mountain terminus near Abergynolwyn, seven

miles distant. En route, passengers can stop off at Dolgoch, a pretty hillside halt shrouded in trees and close to a string of waterfalls. Railway enthusiasts will also want to visit the Narrow Gauge Railway Museum, located at Talyllyn's Tywyn station.

Antiquarian interest in Tywyn centres around a spindly pillar of stone in St Cadfan's Church. Seven feet high, it bears faint traces of what is believed to be the earliest written Welsh, dating probably from the 7th century. This important historic monument is lucky to be here: it was rescued from a farmer's field in which it was reduced to the role of a common gatepost. The little church at Llanegryn, four miles north-east of Tywyn, contains one of Wales's most magnificent rood screens, carved in late medieval times.

TYWYN is on the A493, 19 miles south-west of Dolgellau.

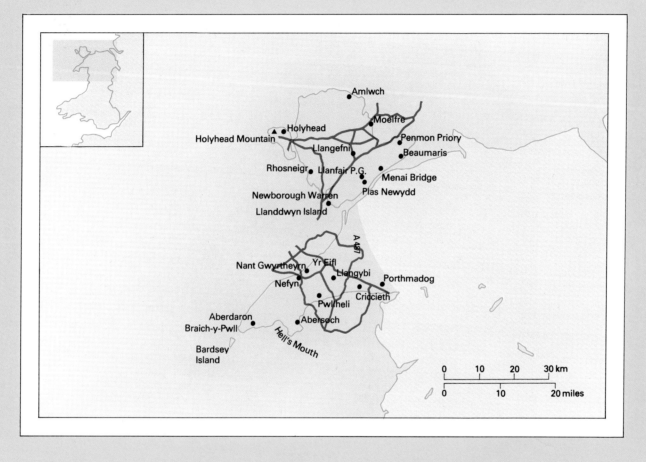

Rock-bound Criccieth Castle stands at the gateway to Lleyn. The rocks become more rugged as the cliffs grow in stature further along this forceful peninsula

ONE IS A RUGGED peninsula, the other a low-lying island. Yet they are the most compatible of neighbours. Both are outposts of North-west Wales, blocked off by Snowdonia. And both are more than grateful to that mountain barrier, for it keeps them away from the mainstream — a distance underlined by Lleyn's isolated, out-on-a-limb location and Anglesey's island status.

The coastlines of both — amounting to around 200 miles in all — are also protected as official 'Areas of Outstanding Natural Beauty'. Lleyn's beauty is a savage, untamed one. Wales's definitive peninsula, it drives dramatically south-westwards into the sea for 24 miles. There is something strongly Celtic about its scattered, whitewashed cottages,

skimpy field-patterns, wind-tangled hedgerows, plunging cliffs and rock-bound shores. In common with Brittany's Finistère and Eire's Kerry, west is the dominant point on the compass.

Anglesey's natural beauty is not nearly as intimidating. This flat island is fringed by a sometimes sandy, sometimes rocky coastline that is positively benign in comparison to its neighbour. The island, known as *Ynys Mon* in Welsh, was a hub of civilization in ancient times and revered as *Mon Mam Cymru* ('The Mother of Wales') because of its fertile farmlands, once the source of so much grain — and also, possibly, due to its importance as a stronghold of Celtic culture before the coming of the Romans.

ABERDARON AND ABERSOCH
Gwynedd

It is possibly provocative, even invidious, to treat these two coastal settlements together, for they are as different as chalk and cheese. Aberdaron, in the remote far west of Lleyn, has until now managed to stand apart from the commercialism and compromises of the outside world.

Overwhelmingly Welsh-speaking and happy to remain so, this little community of stone and lime-washed dwellings crowds into a shallow valley beside a long beach, sheltered from the worst excesses of westerly winds and waves by a cliff-bound headland. Aberdaron, resilient and lonely, almost says something about the Welsh character. The abiding image that lingers in the mind is not of Aberdaron's elemental natural beauty but of its cemetery above the sands which manages to express the Welsh inclination towards bitter-sweet melancholy.

Abersoch is altogether far less weighty and pensive in mood and character. This is where the affluent boating-people congregate. Abersoch harbour, east-facing and sheltered, has developed over the years into a lively sailing and yachting centre as well as a popular little seaside resort.

ABERDARON is at the end of the B4413, approximately 28 miles south-west of Porthmadog. Abersoch, accessible by the A499, is about 19 miles from Porthmadog.

AMLWCH
Gwynedd

This coastal town, in the far north of Anglesey, was the world's busiest copper exporting port in the late 18th century. Amlwch, today a small,

Grey headstones and green headlands gaze down onto the sparse little community at Aberdaron

quite ordinary little place, hardly looks the part. All is explained on its southern approaches, which are dominated by a scarred moonscape. This is Parys Mountain — or, at least, what is left of it after its heyday as Europe's largest copper mining site.

Amlwch, a small-scale seaside and market town, is a good base from which to explore the ruggedly beautiful north Anglesey coast. Neighbouring Bull Bay is popular with cliff walkers and swimmers. Elsewhere, most roads maintain a wary distance from a shoreline which can only properly be explored on foot.

Some of the oldest geological rock formations in the world are to be found along this coast. Evidence of man's influence is scant indeed — apart from one massive exception. Amidst the superb scenic beauty of Wylfa Head, six miles west of Amlwch, a huge nuclear power station has been built. Guided tours are available around a vast, grey complex which is said to be the largest of its kind in the world.

AMLWCH, at the junction of the A5025 and B5111, is 17 miles north-west of Menai Bridge.

BEAUMARIS
Gwynedd

Beaumaris Castle was the final, and in some respects the finest, of the Edwardian fortresses to be built in North Wales. Although the largest of Edward I's castles, it lacks the intimidating presence of its sisters at Conwy and Caernarfon simply because it was never properly finished. Beaumaris comes into its own in pure architectural terms. On the strength of its geometric symmetry, this castle is regarded as the most perfect example of a concentrically planned medieval fortress in Britain.

The castle, dating from 1295, spreads itself out, large, looming and low, in beautiful surroundings at the edge of the town. Those who built it must also have been impressed with its location, giving it the French name of *Beau Marais* ('Beautiful Marsh').

Ring after ring of stone defences radiate outwards from a central core, the whole system presenting a daunting challenge to any would-be attacker. Like most of Edward's castles, Beaumaris was accessible from the sea. The old tidal channel to the Menai Strait has long since disappeared, though the castle's dock — still water-filled, as is part of the moat — survives by the heavily fortified 'Gate Next the Sea', one of the 14 obstacles separating attackers from the inner ward.

Beaumaris itself is a most pleasant seaside town and popular sailing centre, graced with some fine Georgian buildings. There is nothing particularly pleasant about the grimly fascinating Beaumaris Gaol, a Victorian prison, virtually unaltered since its construction in 1829 and now open to visitors.

🚗 *BEAUMARIS, at the junction of the A545 and B5109, is 4 miles northeast of Menai Bridge.*

BRAICH-Y-PWLL AND BARDSEY ISLAND
Gwynedd

Standing on the wind-tossed headland of Braich-y-Pwll contemplating the stormy, dangerous waters of Bardsey Sound, one begins to understand how the medieval pilgrim must have felt. Three pilgrimages to Bardsey, the 'Isle of 20,000 Saints' on which a monastic community had been founded way back in A.D. 615, equalled one to Rome.

The difficulties began when the poor pilgrim, after an undemanding passage along the Lleyn Peninsula, came to face the prospect of crossing the waters to Bardsey, in Welsh *Ynys Enlli*, the 'Isle of the currents' or 'Tide-race island'. Pilgrims braved the hazardous two-mile stretch of Bardsey Sound only after offering prayers for safe passage at the headland Church of St Mary's, the ruins of which can still be made out amongst Braich-y-Pwll's bracken-covered slopes.

Some of the finest coastal views in Britain can be enjoyed from the 524-ft summit of Braich-y-Pwll, the 'Land's End of North Wales'. The land ends very abruptly indeed, plunging down from the viewpoint onto a curtain of jagged sea-cliffs.

Bardsey Sound still causes problems. The island, now privately owned by an environmental trust, is regularly cut off for days.

🚗 *BRAICH-Y-PWLL (a steep road winds its way right to the summit) is accessible by minor road off the B4413, 2½ miles south-west of Aberdaron.*

Beaumaris Castle's stunted, incomplete defences overlook the Menai Strait

91

CRICCIETH
Gwynedd

Criccieth's castle really looks as though it has been in the wars. Appearances are not deceptive. The castle's ruined walls and ragged towers (there are even scorchmarks to be seen here) testify to an action-packed past. Dating from around 1230, this stronghold has, in its time, been in both Welsh and English hands. The *coup de grâce* was delivered in 1404, when the castle was sacked and burnt by Welsh leader Owain Glyndwr, never to recover.

The castle sits on top of the grassy headland which separates Criccieth's twin beaches. As a seaside resort, Criccieth is deliberately unspectacular, preferring the role of a staid, appealingly traditional Welsh watering place not too concerned with fashion or passing fads.

The village of Llanystumdwy, two miles to the west, was the boyhood home of that charismatic political figure, Liberal M.P. and Prime Minister, David Lloyd George.

The 'Welsh Wizard', although born in Manchester (in 1863), was brought up from 1864 to 1880 in this quiet little village. A slate plaque identifies his humble home, a terraced cottage which stands a few doors from a museum dedicated to his memory. Lloyd George died in 1945 and is buried at Llanystumdwy.

CRICCIETH, at the junction of the A497 and B4411, is 4 miles west of Porthmadog.

HELL'S MOUTH
Gwynedd

Nineteenth-century sailors were in no doubt that this rock-bound bay, between Aberdaron and Abersoch, justified its name. Hell's Mouth (its Welsh name of Porth Neigwl is not a translation) takes a giant-sized bite out of Lleyn's south-western tip. On a sunny, still day, this empty four-mile-long bay looks benign enough. But its exposed waters are deceptive and volatile, with a savage reputation as a graveyard for many a vessel.

One of its most famous wrecks was that of *The Twelve Apostles* in 1898. In keeping with local legends, the ship was drawn siren-like to her doom despite every effort made by the crew to change course.

The densely wooded hillside above the north-western corner of the bay conceals Plas-yn-Rhiw (a National Trust property). This small manor house, medieval in origin with Tudor and Georgian additions, has a wonderfully profuse garden in which shrubs, trees, rhododenrons, azaleas and sub-tropical species flourish in apparent abandon.

HELL'S MOUTH, about 21 miles south-west of Porthmadog, is accessible by minor road between Abersoch and Aberdaron.

HOLYHEAD AND HOLYHEAD MOUNTAIN
Gwynedd

This busy port and holiday centre stands on an island-off-an-island. Holyhead Island is connected to the Isle of Anglesey by two road bridges and a rail link. All routes seem to lead to Holyhead. With the completion of the London to Holyhead road — now the A5 — by Thomas Telford in the early 19th century, a port grew up here serving the Irish cross-channel route (ferries still sail to Dun Laoghaire, near Dublin).

Nineteenth-century engineers were by no means the first to appreciate Holyhead's fine harbour. The Romans constructed a rectangular fort, *Caer Gybi*, here, probably as a base for a small naval flotilla which protected the Welsh coast from Irish raiders.

Caer Gybi ('Cybi's Fort') takes its name from the 6th-century saint who settled within its abandoned walls. These walls, which survive to reasonable height and display the 'herringbone masonry' typical of the late Roman period, now surround the Church of St Cybi in the centre of Holyhead.

The Holyhead Mountain Hut Circles, in the rugged terrain west of the town, are the remnants of a large native farming settlement that existed here in Roman times. The slopes are scattered with circular hut foundations, some of which retain their original hearths and slab beds.

Caer y Twr Hill Fort stands right on the 720-ft summit of the mountain, overlooking Holyhead Bay and the Irish Sea. The climb is well worth it, not only for the views. This Iron Age stronghold was later improved by the Romans, who made good use of the site as a look-out point. Remnants from those far-off days have not entirely disappeared, for Caer y Twr still retains its sentry walk amongst well laid out remains.

On the far west of the island, mountain meets sea at the South Stack lighthouse. Over 400 steps zigzag down the cliffs to the lighthouse, perched on a rock amongst magnificent coastal scenery. The cliffs here (an R.S.P.B. reserve) are noted for their colonies of sea-birds, especially guillemots, razorbills and puffins, a birdwatcher's paradise.

HOLYHEAD, accessible by the A5 or B4545, is 17 miles north-west of Menai Bridge.

A dizzy staircase leads across to South Stack lighthouse, guardian of the western approach to Holyhead Island

LLANFAIR P.G.
Gwynedd

It is quite impossible for any Welsh travel book to get away without listing Llanfair P.G.'s name in its full glory. So here goes: - Llanfairpwllgwyngyllgogerychwyrn-drobwllllantysiliogogogoch. The locals have long since abbreviated it to a more manageable Llanfair P.G. Those fascinated by this, the longest — and most prosaic — place-name in the world, will want to know that it

means 'St Mary's (Church) by the white aspen over the whirlpool and St Tysilio's (Church) by the red cave'. Visitors flock here to have their photographs taken next to the name (bring a wide-angled camera) which appears in its full unpronounceable glory on the railway station and the frontages of one or two of the local businesses.

In fields just over one mile south-west of the village lies one of Anglesey's — and Britain's — most evocative prehistoric sites. A narrow

stone doorway set into a round, grass-covered mound leads through a cramped underground passage into the central tomb of Bryn Celli Ddu, a burial chamber built as a site of pagan ritual around 3000 to 3500 B.C. Along with Barclodiad y Gawres (see Rhosneigr entry), this tomb is one of the few in Britain that revealed evidence of prehistoric rock art when excavated.

LLANFAIR P.G., at the junction of the A5, A4080, and B5420 is 1½ miles west of Menai Bridge.

LLANGEFNI
Gwynedd

Inland Anglesey is at its flattest and most featureless around centrally located Llangefni. The surroundings do little to enhance the appeal of a town with no great deal of character — as one would expect of a place mainly notable as the administrative 'capital' of the island.

Anglesey's farmlands, at one time 'the granary of Wales', have now switched from arable to pastoral use.

94   **A prehistoric graveyard. In the megalithic age, man buried his dead in communal chambers such as Bryn Celli Ddu**

Llangefni is at its most animated in its role as a busy market centre when the farmers get together here for the livestock sales every Wednesday and Thursday.

The Bodeilio Weaving Centre at Talwrn, a mile or so north-east of Llangefni, is well worth a detour. Beautifully renovated farm buildings house a museum and crafts gallery that, with the assistance of practical demonstrations, trace the history of early textile production with particular emphasis on handweaving.

LLANGEFNI, at the junction of the A5114, B5109, B5110 and B5111, is approximately 8 miles north-west of Menai Bridge.

LLANGYBI
Gwynedd

Llangybi, in the middle of nowhere in particular, is not the sort of place that immediately catches the eye. The trip along Lleyn's back lanes is justified by the presence here of an enchanting holy well. The claimed curative powers of Ffynnon Gybi, St Cybi's Well, could almost come from the silence and simplicity of this lovely site, traditionally associated with the 6th-century saint who travelled widely throughout Wales.

A short walk past the village church leads down into a secluded little valley and the ruins of a rough stone cottage and walls. The latter enclose the cool waters of the well, an evocative place of pilgrimage for hundreds of years.

LLANGYBI, on a minor road 6 miles north-east of Pwllheli, is most easily accessible off the A499.

Engineer and bridge-builder Thomas Telford excelled himself when faced with the challenge of crossing the Menai Strait

MENAI BRIDGE
Gwynedd

This little Isle of Angelsey town lives under the elegant shadow of its famous road bridge, constructed by that great engineer Thomas Telford in the 1820s. Telford's bridge — the world's first iron suspension bridge — was the last link in the London to Holyhead (and Dublin) route. One thousand feet long, with a main span of 579 ft, it cleverly takes advantage of a narrow channel where the waters of the Menai Strait curl around a wooded promontory.

The symmetrical bridge blends well with the natural beauty of its surroundings. As an exercise in design and decoration, it stands as an interesting comparison to the recent Britannia Road Bridge, built just to the west to relieve the traffic congestion inevitably experienced when the Menai Bridge's narrow portals were the only entry and exit points to the Isle of Anglesey.

MENAI BRIDGE, near the junction of the A5, A545, and A5025, is 8 miles north-east of Caernarfon.

MOELFRE
Gwynedd

On the east coast of Anglesey, this charming little village with its small harbour, pebble beach and lifeboat station looks distinctly Cornish in character. Those in search of a proper beach must journey across the headland to Traeth Lligwy (Lligwy Bay), a beautiful and expansive stretch of sands.

A clutch of memorable historic sites spanning over 4000 years are grouped together amongst fields and woodlands close to the sea. Lligwy Cromlech is colossal. A weather-beaten 28-ton capstone rests on a series of low upright stone supports, the entire framework of this neolithic (New Stone Age) burial chamber exposed to the skies. Originally, the cromlech would have been covered by a large cairn to create an underground vault in which prehistoric farmers laid their dead. Excavations in 1908 unearthed the bones of 30 people, together with examples of Neolithic and early Bronze Age pottery.

A short walk into the woods leads to an extensive collection of stones which, even on first impressions, obviously have a certain order to them. Closer inspection reveals the plan of an ancient village known as Din Lligwy. Visible remains — stout stone walls enclosing a group of huts still standing six feet high in places — probably relate to the Roman period, though the village is thought to date from nearly 3000 years ago.

The story of man's influence on this remote hillside continues at Capel Lligwy, a ruined 12th-century chapel partly restored in the 14th and 16th centuries.

MOELFRE, accessible by the A5025 and A5108, is 10 miles north of Menai Bridge.

NANT GWYRTHEYRN
Gwynedd

According to legend, Vortigen, the 5th-century king said to have invited the Saxons to Britain, paid for his deed by becoming a fugitive and dying in this 'gloomy hollow' of a valley. Nant Gwyrtheyrn, a shadowy, inaccessible vale below the Yr Eifl mountains and just off the saints' route to Bardsey Island, is certainly one of the most eerie places on Lleyn, a location where landscape fits legend perfectly.

Nant Gwyrtheyrn's highly charged atmosphere does not diminish when the valley opens out to the sea and a few rows of cottages come into view. This is the 'ghost village' of Porth-y-nant, finally abandoned in the 1950s after the closure of the quarries that had supplied its lifeblood.

One can understand why the villagers left. Supplies to this isolated settlement had to be brought in by sea. The only way down to this bleak but hauntingly beautiful spot is by foot, along a steep path cut into the slopes of Nant Gwyrtheyrn. New life is now being injected into Porth-y-nant. Some of the derelict dwellings have been renovated for use as a Welsh language studies centre.

NANT GWYRTHEYRN and Porth-y-nant are accessible by footpath from a car park 1 mile north of Llithfaen, a village on the B4417 16 miles south-west of Caernarfon.

NEFYN
Gwynedd

Nefyn and its neighbouring bays are a classic case of what might have been. This area would have changed beyond recognition had an ambitious 19th-century plan come to fruition. The scheme involved turning Porth Dinllaen — a few miles to the west

A curving bay on the Lleyn Peninsula at Nefyn

and the only safe anchorage on this stretch of coast — into a full-scale cross-channel port serving the London to Dublin route.

Similar plans for Holyhead found greater favour, leaving the bay of Porth Dinllaen untouched and pretty as a picture. A cluster of whitewashed cottages huddle beneath a protective headland at the end of a perfect crescent of sands, a scene made doubly welcoming by its interruption of the stark, forbidding cliff scenery typical of Lleyn's north-facing coastline.

Porth Nefyn, next door, is a smaller version of its neighbour. The excellent beach here has been in-strumental in the development of Nefyn as a popular little seaside resort, the only one along this stretch of the peninsula.

Breaches in the cliffs along northern Lleyn are indeed infrequent. Sandy beaches are something of a rarity, one of the few being Porth Oer, about 12 miles south-west of Nefyn. This little bay is perhaps better known as 'Whistling Sands', thus named because its sand granules are supposed to whistle or squeak underfoot.

NEFYN, where the A497 meets the B4417, is 19 miles south-west of Caernarfon.

Beautiful Llanddwyn on the Isle of Anglesey, capped by a stubby little lighthouse

NEWBOROUGH WARREN AND LLANDDWYN ISLAND
Gwynedd

Anglesey's south-western extremity is a strange combination of dunelands, beaches, pine forests, salt marsh and sea-rocks, capped by an isolated promontory lighthouse. The vast expanses of deserted dunes at the nature reserve of Newborough Warren are a haven for a wide variety of wild flowers and fauna. Newborough Forest, next door, is a large conifer plantation stretching right down to the lonely sands along Llanddwyn Bay.

From the forest car park, a path leads across to Llanddwyn Island, a rocky, narrow promontory cut off only at high tide. Its ruined church is dedicated to St Dwynwen, a 5th-century saint who lived here. A stubby little lighthouse overlooks much more than the western approach to the Menai Strait. It commands truly splendid views down the long arm of the Lleyn Peninsula and up into the gritty purple heights of Snowdonia.

THIS AREA is accessible by minor road leading south-west from Newborough, a village on the A4080 10 miles south-west of Menai Bridge.

PENMON PRIORY
Gwynedd

The Augustinian Priory of Penmon, near the eastern tip of Anglesey and approach to the Menai Strait, is a site of great antiquity. It was probably founded in the 6th century by St Cynlas, who subsequently passed it on to his brother, St Seiriol. As we see it now, Penmon — much raided by the marauding Vikings during the Dark Ages — dates mainly from the 12th and 13th centuries.

A ruined priory range, a large building with cellar, refectory and

97

Holiday craft in Porthmadog harbour today occupy berths previously used by slate traders

dormitory, stands right next to a medieval place of worship, still in use as the parish church. A holy well and dovecot, both located nearby, complete the scene. The latter, built c.1600 with a domed stone roof which holds nearly 1000 birds, is particularly impressive. From Penmon, it is only a short drive to Penmon Point on the far east of Anglesey which overlooks Puffin Island, another early Christian settlement.

PENMON is accessible by the B5109 and minor road, 4 miles north-east of Beaumaris.

PLAS NEWYDD
Gwynedd

The wooden leg used by the 1st Marquess of Anglesey is one of the more unorthodox relics on view in this splendid house located on the banks of the Menai Strait. 'The Anglesey leg', one of the first articulated artificial limbs to be invented, was used by the Marquess after he was dismembered in the Battle of Waterloo. The replacement now stands, amongst other memorabilia, in the Cavalry Museum.

Plas Newydd, a National Trust property, is more conventionally famous for its Rex Whistler Room which contains a wall painting that puts cinemascope to shame. Painted by Whistler between 1936 and 1940, this 58-ft canvas depicts with great flourish a mountain-backed coastline — in no way representational but surely an echo of the view across the Menai Strait to Snowdonia — on which imaginary buildings straight out of renaissance Italy bask in warm southern sunshine. Whistler's mural is considered to be the finest wall painting in any country house in Britain.

Five-hundred-year-old Plas Newydd ('The New Place') hardly lives up to its name. As it stands now, though, the house — an elegant Georgian Gothick one and largely the work of architect James Wyatt — dates from the late 18th century. It stands amongst grassy slopes, woodlands and gardens in a 169-acre estate leading down to the banks of the Menai Strait.

PLAS NEWYDD is accessible off the A4080, 3 miles south-west of Menai Bridge.

PORTHMADOG
Gwynedd

One hundred years ago, Porthmadog's harbourside would have looked very different. Tall-masted brigs, ketches and schooners then lined its quay, waiting to take on cargoes of fine Welsh slate for shipment to other parts of Britain and overseas.

Sleek yachts and holiday craft have now taken over, and a swish, marina-style housing complex shares the harbour with the old, stone-built wharfside warehouses. Nevertheless, Porthmadog's links with the past largely define the present, especially at the Ffestiniog Railway, arguably the most attractive of the many narrow-gauge 'Great Little Trains of Wales'.

The Ffestiniog was built in 1836 to carry slate from the caverns at Blaenau Ffestiniog to Porthmadog harbour. Nowadays, it transports tourists along a truly delightful and scenic route that begins on the water's edge and ends deep in the mountains, 12 miles distant.

One of the most memorable sections of line comes immediately after the Porthmadog terminus, where the railway crosses the tidal sweep of

Traeth Bach — the confluence of the Glaslyn and Dwyryd estuaries — on a mile-long embankment known locally as The Cob. This was built by William Madocks (1773-1828), a dynamic entrepreneur responsible for shaping much of Porthmadog's past.

Madocks makes an appearance on a huge and heroic wall mural that, as well as depicting the port's history, attracts the summer visitors to the site of Porthmadog Pottery. More history resides along the quay at an unusual maritime museum that is part afloat, part on terra firma. The main 'exhibit' is the *S.S. Garlandstone*, an old sailing ketch moored next to the museum's quayside exhibition hall.

A second enthusiasts' railway is also based at Porthmadog. It is early days yet, though, for the Welsh Highland Railway, which currently runs for only a short distance towards its eventual goal, the Aberglaslyn Pass.

PORTHMADOG is on the A497, 21 miles south-east of Caernarfon.

PWLLHELI
Gwynedd

All that the Victorian guidebooks — not noted for their reticent descriptions — could find to say about Pwllheli was that 'the staple delicacies of the neighbourhood — fried sole and duck — may be most comfortably discussed in its excellent hotels'. Faint praise indeed for a place, admittedly not in the mainstream of Welsh tourism, which boasts an excellent, undeservedly unpatronized beach and fine, sheltered harbour.

Much-mispronounced Pwllheli, the main market town for the area, is also conveniently situated for those wishing to explore the Lleyn Peninsula. Its station is the end of the line for the Cambrian Coast railway, one

Blaenau Ffestiniog slate, transported to Porthmadog, was the original payload on the Ffestiniog Railway

of British Rail's most scenic services, which runs along Tremadog and Cardigan Bays all the way to Aberystwyth.

Pennarth Fawr, on a minor road four miles to the north-east (and signposted off the A497), is a real rarity: an early 15th-century stone-built hall house, one of the few surviving in Wales.

🚗 *PWLLHELI, at the junction of the A497 and A499, is 12 miles west of Porthmadog and 21 miles south-west of Caernarfon on the A499.*

RHOSNEIGR
Gwynedd

A lovely sweep of breezy sands, string of bays and acres of dunes attract visitors to this small resort on Anglesey's west coast. Rhosneigr is almost surrounded by water — saltwater to the west, and the large freshwater lake of Llyn Maelog just inland behind the houses.

The headland of Porth Trecastell, one-and-a-half miles to the south, is a prehistoric graveyard. Barclodiad y Gawres ('The Giantess's Apronful') is one of the most significant of the many ancient burial chambers on the island. Five of its stones are decorated with carved patterns, rare examples of prehistoric tomb art. Unlike most of its stark, bare-stoned contemporaries, Barclodiad y Gawres has been extensively restored and covered over once more. A 20-ft-long passageway leads to a renovated, cross-shaped central chamber which, when excavated in the 1950s, revealed cremated human bones.

Today, one would hardly associate royal splendour and courtly life with the village of Aberffraw, four miles south-east of Rhosneigr. Yet up until the 13th-century conquest of Wales by Edward I, this inconspicuous place served as the seat of government of the Welsh princes.

🚗 *RHOSNEIGR, on the A4080, is approximately 16 miles west of Menai Bridge.*

YR EIFL
Gwynedd

The Yr Eifl mountains (anglicized to 'The Rivals') are a trio of peaks rising to 1850 ft, the highest point on Lleyn. They look as though they should be even higher, for their altitude is magnified by their location, right next to the sea. From the shores around Trefor they soar up almost vertically from the ocean as a massive buttress of land.

Lleyn is littered with prehistoric remains, none finer than those on Yr Eifl. Iron Age man, always drawn to high ground, settled amongst the rock and boulder-strewn eastern summit. His encampment, known as Tre'r Ceiri ('The Town of the Giants'), is very well preserved indeed. This was much more than a simple hill fort. Wall defences — still standing 13 ft high in places — enclose a complete township of around 150 huts which was lived in up until the time of the Roman occupation of Wales.

🚗 *YR EIFL lies between Llanaelhaearn and Llithfaen along Lleyn's north-facing coast, about 16 miles south-west of Caernarfon.*

Seascape at Porth Trecastell, a prehistoric graveyard near Rhosneigr, Anglesey. Many ancient burial chambers can be found on the island

Myths and Legends

Wales's misty mountains, gloomy defiles and haunting hillsides have been a potent breeding ground for myths and legends since the times when tales were passed on, word-of-mouth, from fireside to fireside; aided and abetted, no doubt, by the Welsh gift for storytelling.

Celtic folk tales, their roots thousands of years old, would have been told in the courts of the Welsh princes. They were written for the first time in manuscript form in the early 14th century. The collection became known as the *Mabinogion*, an everyday story of heroism and murder, romance and treachery, magic and the mutation of man to beast in the Celtic Wales of yesterday.

The action in this picaresque collection took place throughout the country, especially in Pembrokeshire, the *Mabinogion's Gwlad hud a lledrith* ('The land of magic and enchantment').

North Wales is evoked powerfully in the 'Dream of Mascen Wledig' who, on coming to Caernarfon, 'could see a great castle, the fairest that mortal had ever seen'. In this case, folklore may well have been founded in fact, for Mascen was Magnus Maximus, the Roman emperor who travelled to his fort at Segontium, alias Caernarfon.

Other tales tax the belief of even the most credulous. Serpents appear from the waves and victims are swallowed by witches to be re-born omniscient babies. Wales, along with the rest of Britain, also claims its cast-iron Arthurian connections. Those in search of the elusive

Devil's Bridge has legendary connections with Satan

Camelot need look no further than Caerleon, quite obviously his court because it was 'the most accessible place in his dominions'. Merlin's Oak in Carmarthen and a pile of 'Arthur's Stones' scattered across Wales either confirm or contradict the legend — depending upon which side of the fence you happen to stand.

Mythology is by no means confined to the *Mabinogion*. Places all over Wales, such as Devil's Bridge, have their own local tales to tell. Lakes have always provided a powerful stimulus to story-telling, typical of which is the tale of the maiden who emerges from the waters to marry the farmer only to vanish after some chance misunderstanding (as at Llyn-y-

Fan-Fach in the Brecon Beacons).

Not even Christopher Columbus is safe from such speculations. The Welsh, of course, were responsible for discovering America thanks to Prince Madoc (1150-80) who set sail from North Wales with ten ships. The fact that he was never seen again might confirm or contradict the legend . . .

MAY HEAV'N PROTECT OUR HOME FROM FLAME,
OR HURT OR HARM OF VARIOUS NAME!
AND MAY NO EVIL LUCK BETIDE
TO ANY WHO THEREIN ABIDE!
AS ALSO WHO THEIR HOMES HAVE FOUND
ON ANY ACRE OF IT'S GROUND,
OR WHO FROM HOMES BEYOND IT'S GATE
BESTOW THEIR TOIL ON THIS ESTATE!

—P.Y.

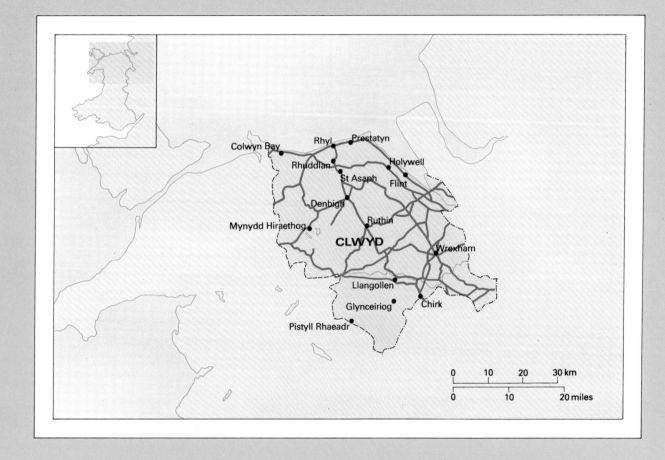

A scene from the servant's quarters at Erddig Hall, part of the social history of Wales

THE COUNTY OF CLWYD, a geographically convenient entity, fits the north-east corner of Wales like a glove. Two of its main features are the eponymous Vale of Clwyd and Clwydian Hills.

Clwyd is a mixed bag of influences. There are one or two large towns here, a counterpoint to delightful medieval settlements such as Ruthin and Denbigh, full of architectural heritage. Fertile vales, where the farming is rich and productive, shelter beneath inviolate hill country in which sheep farmers maintain a hold that is no more than tenuous. Wild moorland subsides to settled coastline in the north, a sandy strip of seashore which meets the Dee estuary at the Point of Ayr.

The Clwydian Hills, a natural east-west barrier, rise to 1817 ft at Moel Famau above a pastoral valley watered by the River Clwyd. Further west the uplands between the Vales of Clwyd and Conwy are filled with the moody moors, huge lakes and forests of Mynydd Hiraethog.

Mynydd Hiraethog dips down to the sea along a shoreline of familiar resorts which continue to serve as mainstays of the traditional holiday trade. An entirely different seascape resides beyond the Point of Ayr, where many species of wading birds breed amongst empty tidal sands.

South of Hiraethog, the typical Welsh landscape of green valleys and remote mountains once more takes over. Beyond the lovely Vale of Llangollen, the Berwyn Mountains rise to a 2713-ft high point, embracing within their folds Pistyll Rhaeadr, the loftiest waterfall in Wales.

CHIRK
Clwyd

Chirk is the home of a magnificent National Trust property. Chirk Castle, one mile west of the little town, is a rare example of an austere medieval stronghold that has evolved, over the years, into a sumptuous stately home.

The secret of Chirk's success lies in its longevity. Amongst North Wales's many fortresses, this castle is unique in having been occupied continuously from medieval times to the present day. Chirk began life in the late 13th century as a castle put up to consolidate Edward I's hold on Wales. It was bought in 1595 by Sir Thomas Myddleton, a merchant adventurer who sailed with Sir Walter Raleigh, and has been the home of the Myddleton family ever since.

Inevitably, Chirk has seen much alteration — its interiors, for example, are mostly 17th, 18th and 19th century. The incongruity of an erstwhile medieval fort surrounded by landscaped gardens and a splendid 468-acre park is not lost on the visitor.

Within its solid walls, more splendour reigns. Chirk really came of age in the 1760s, when the series of Neo-Classical state rooms were created. Along with the Neo-Gothic additions of the 19th century — the oak panelled entrance hall is particularly fine — these luxuriously furnished and decorated rooms represent Chirk's greatest glories.

Despite such opulence, many visitors come to Chirk just to see the gates. Made by the Davies brothers of Bersham, near Wrexham, in 1719-21, they are an unrivalled achievement, a work of art executed in iron to an impossibly delicate and ornate design, and finished in black and gold.

Castle is separated from town by the Shropshire Union Canal and railway. The former spans the valley

104 **Faint traces of military authority linger as reminders that the stately home of Chirk originated as a border stronghold**

at the foot of Chirk on a fine Thomas Telford aqueduct of the late 18th century, an engineering feat imitated in 1848 by its neighbouring railway viaduct.

🚗 CHIRK, at the junction of the A483 and B4500, is 10 miles south of Wrexham.

COLWYN BAY
Clwyd

It is interesting — and often wildly amusing — to read what the old guidebooks have to say about the Welsh seaside resorts. Colwyn Bay's climate, according to one early tome, is 'said to resemble that of the Riviera, without the intense heat, or that of Japan, without the rain'.

Quite how many Victorian tourists were able to travel to the Orient — or the Mediterranean for that matter — to verify this claim is not known. Today's visitors to this cheerful and spacious resort bring with them a less optimistic view of British weather, which assumes tangible form in the shape of the inevitable plastic mac.

Colwyn Bay, along with Llandudno, Rhyl and Prestatyn, make up North Wales's quartet of long-established traditional seaside resorts. Apart from the predictable features of promenade, beach and rorty amusements, it boasts a fine pier — an increasingly cherished piece of seaside architecture, and rightly so — and a well laid out Mountain Zoo in the wooded hillsides high above the resort.

🚗 COLWYN BAY is accessible off the A55 approximately 39 miles west of Chester.

DENBIGH
Clwyd

Denbigh's hilltop castle, conspicuous against its blackcloth of the Clwydian Hills, tends to capture the limelight — to the detriment of another medieval feature, a well preserved but largely ignored series of town walls, which plunge and climb around this hilly, complicated old settlement in an almost complete circuit.

Both castle and walls occupy the centre stage of Welsh history. Denbigh was a nucleus of Welsh resistance to the English invasion of the late 13th century. By 1282 it had fallen into the hands of Henry de Lacy, cohort of the English king, Edward I. Work then began on constructing the castle, on the site of the former Welsh native stronghold.

Denbigh's ruinous state is hardly surprising, considering its turbulent past. Captured by the Welsh in 1294 and later retaken, it was also involved in the Owain Glyndwr uprising of the 15th century, the Wars of the Roses and the Civil War. Its strongest feature is undoubtedly the Great Gatehouse, a huge triangular defence with a trio of interlinked octagonal towers. Look out for the niche which contains a statue, probably that of Edward I.

Denbigh Friary, on the eastern outskirts of town, is a small and simple 14th-century monastic house with a chequered history.

🚗 DENBIGH, between Ruthin and Rhyl, is at the junction of the A525 and A543.

FLINT
Clwyd

Do not avoid this admittedly very ordinary Deeside town. Flint comes to life for the visitor only because of its castle, historically and symbolically most significant as the first of Edward I's chain of mighty 13th-century fortresses built in North Wales to subdue and contain the unruly Welsh.

Urban development has not been kind to Flint Castle. Its once magisterial position has been destroyed by the modern town — indeed, it is quite easy to miss completely. The castle, dating from 1277, is worth seeking out if only for its Great Tower, or donjon, a large, isolated round tower, set apart as a last defence, looking out to sea.

Flint Castle, thanks to William Shakespeare's efforts in his third act of Richard II, is forever remembered as the setting for the final capture of Richard in 1399.

🚗 FLINT, at the junction of the A548 and A5119, is about 15 miles north-west of Wrexham.

Amongst Chirk's most remarkable features are the Davies brothers' wrought iron entrance gates

GLYNCEIRIOG
Clwyd

Off-the-beaten-track Glynceiriog hides itself in a great bend in the Ceiriog Valley. Motorists unafraid of shudderingly steep mountain roads should do as the locals do and take the short cut (as opposed to the long way around via Chirk) to Llangollen: an as-the-crow-flies route which climbs out of the village and across a shoulder of the Berwyn Mountains before dropping into the Vale of Dee.

Before leaving this secluded settlement, visitors should experience something of its industrial past. Records show that slate was quarried here as early as the 9th century, though the heaps of spoil from the old mines are now hidden by trees and wild flowers.

The old Chwarel Wynne slate cavern, evocatively advertised as 'the lost cavern of Glynceiriog', has found a new role for itself since reopening for guided tours in the 1970s. In comparison to the vast underground workings elsewhere in North Wales — especially at Blaenau Ffestiniog, the former 'slate capital' — this cavern is quite small: in its heyday at the turn of the century, it only employed 77 men. Chwarel Wynne's modest size and relative obscurity (Blaenau Ffestiniog's well publicised caverns can become very busy in summer) work to its advantage, visitors benefitting from a more personal conducted tour as they walk down into the first and second-level chambers of the mine.

◣ *GLYNCEIRIOG, at the junction of the B4500 and B4579, is 7 miles west of Chirk.*

St Winifride's Well. A somewhat sanctimonious Dr Johnson criticised its bathing arrangements

HOLYWELL
Clwyd

This small township owes its name and fame to St Winifride's Well, variously described as one of Wales's 'Seven Wonders' and — more aptly, perhaps — the 'Lourdes of Wales'. Possibly the most famous healing well in Britain, St Winifride's dates from the 7th century when, according to a bloody Celtic folk tale recorded in a book printed by William Caxton in 1485, poor Winifride's head 'was cut off and touchyd the ground (where) sprang up a welle of spryngyng water . . . which heleth al langours . . .'

The shrine has now been a place of pilgrimage for well over 1000 years. Services are still held at the elaborate Well Chapel, built over the waters in perpendicular Gothic style in the late 15th century. A disapproving Dr Johnson noted in 1774 that 'the bath is completely and indecently open: a woman bathed while we all looked on.'

The shallow vale leading for over a mile from the town to the Dee estuary has in recent years been designated the Greenfield Valley Heritage Park. Two hundred years ago, this now tranquil stretch of lakeside and woodland walks was a hive of industrial activity. A number of old buildings survive from the times when textiles, copper and brass were produced here in abundance. The estuary end of the valley is marked by the ruins of Basingwerk Abbey, a monastery founded in 1131 by the French Savignac order and later taken over by the sheep-rearing Cistercians.

The Grange Cavern Military Museum is worth visiting for the setting alone: a chilly, gloomy two-and-a-half acre cavern, hollowed out of the hillside above Holywell, which contains over 70 military vehicles including tanks, jeeps and artillery. With such a distinct dearth of subterranean competitors, no one can possibly doubt its claim to the title of 'the world's largest underground military museum'.

🚗 *HOLYWELL is at the junction of the A55, A5026 and B5121, approximately 19 miles north-west of Wrexham.*

LLANGOLLEN
Clwyd

Llangollen is a little town with a big personality. Its name has been spread worldwide thanks to the prestigious International Musical Eisteddfod held here each July. Unlike other eisteddfodau (see special feature, page 109), Llangollen's looks outside Wales.

First held in 1947 to help heal the wounds of war, the event attracts up to 15,000 musicians and dancers every year from over 30 nations. Performers from countries as disparate as Czechoslovakia, Bangladesh and Japan meet and compete here, their traditional folk costumes bringing a cosmopolitan splash of colour to the streets of this Welsh town.

Exuberant 'magpie' architecture at Llangollen's Plas Newydd, below the ruins of Castell Dinas Bran

Llangollen lies in a deep and protective valley beside the rushing waters of the River Dee, only a few miles from the flat English borderlands but well insulated from them by enveloping mountains. Castell Dinas Bran stands 1000 ft high on one mountain crest, its stumpy ruins casting a weathered eye over the town.

This 13th-century Welsh native stronghold was probably built by Madog, Prince of Powys. Four centuries earlier, Cyngen, another Prince of Powys, erected Eliseg's Pillar in memory of his great-grandfather. The pillar, set on its original mound, is one mile north of Llangollen near the grand loop of the Horseshoe Pass, a road that frequently succumbs to winter snows. Close by are the extensive remains of Valle Crucis Abbey, a Cistercian house founded in 1201 by Prince Madog's father.

A trio of landmarks are located within the town itself. Llangollen grew up around its handsome stone bridge, medieval in origin, and one of the 'Seven Wonders of Wales', an accolade which should not be taken too seriously (see Wrexham entry).

The most talked about inhabitants of the town were undoubtedly the 'Ladies of Llangollen', Lady Eleanor Butler, her companion the Hon. Sarah Ponsonby and their maid Mary Carryll (also known apparently as Molly the Basher). From 1780, they set up a highly eccentric home here which was visited by many luminaries of the time, including Shelley, Byron and Wordsworth. Their black-and-white timbered mansion, its interior displaying a wealth of oak carving, is open to the public. Llangollen Canal, a branch of the Shropshire Union, has inspired the establishment of the Canal Exhibition Centre, an imaginative museum housed beside the town wharf in an

Cruising 120ft above ground on the Llangollen Canal's Pontcysyllte aqueduct, the longest in Britain

early 19th-century warehouse.

🦢 *LLANGOLLEN, at the junction of the A5, A539 and A542, is 10 miles south-west of Wrexham.*

MYNYDD HIRAETHOG
Clwyd

The heather covered moorlands west of Ruthin occupy an emotional position in traditional Welsh culture. No equivalent single word exists in the English language which captures the full meaning of *hiraethog*. The nearest approximations are 'homesick' and 'longing', a reflection of the rich seam of history and heritage that underlies Hiraethog's now-empty moorlands.

Where man once lived there are now conifer trees and reservoirs. The Clocaenog Forest, Wales's second largest plantation, clothes much of the southern and eastern moor (at Bod Petrual, just off the B5105, an

old gamekeeper's cottage has been converted into an interesting and attractive Forest Visitor Centre).

The most recent man-made addition is Llyn Brenig, a wide, squat sheet of water — over 13,000 million gallons in all — in the central moor. Completed in 1976, Brenig joins Llyn Alwen, a smaller reservoir built here in the early 1900s. Both are surrounded by Hiraethog's soft, rounded outlines — a deceptive landscape, for this is high, bleak and windy country, consistently over the 1000 ft contour line, and fiercely cold in winter.

Although now unpopulated, Hiraethog was settled for many thousands of years. Mystery surrounds many of the prehistoric sites here, though those excavated around the reservoir reveal definitive evidence of mesolithic (Middle Stone Age) and Bronze Age man. In medieval times, hafodydd were constructed here (a *hafod* is a summer

camp or house, built by those tending flocks of sheep and cattle brought to the moorlands for summer grazing), perpetuating a tradition of transhumance — that is, moving from 'moor to shore' according to the seasons — established by prehistoric man. From these scattered settlements and the shared hardships of living on Mynydd Hiraethog sprang a rich culture, as shepherds met to create their own entertainment at *noson lawen*, evenings of song and poetry.

The history and ecology of this fascinating and unique part of North Wales is told at the excellent Brenig Visitor Centre, located at the dam. This centre is the starting point for a number of lakeside footpaths, one of which leads to the excavated archaeological sites.

🦢 *MYNYDD HIRAETHOG is bounded by the towns of Ruthin, Denbigh and Llanrwst, with the A5 running along its southern boundary.*

Eisteddfodau explained – a 2000-year tradition

Bardic ritual at the Royal National Eisteddfod

The International Eisteddfod

The tradition of the eisteddfod — a competitive event in literature, music and the arts, held in the Welsh language — can be traced back to 1176 when the Lord Rhys ap Gruffudd held a Christmastide gathering at Cardigan. Within courtly circles in medieval Wales, the skills of the bard (or poet) were much revered. Events which put those talents to the test soon became popular, most notably at Carmarthen in the early 1450s when the term *eisteddfod* was first coined.

By the 16th century, eisteddfodau had begun to fall into the doldrums. The movement was re-awoken — some would say re-invented — thanks in part to the fertile imagination of one man, Iolo Morgannwg.

Iolo began life, in 1747, as plain and simple Edward Williams. A great self-publicist, he soon transformed his identity into a bardic one. Iolo's romantic obsession with druidic civilization in Britain before the coming of the Romans and Saxons, together with his showmanship and suspect skills as an historian led to the creation of 'The Gorsedd of the Bards'.

Although a pure invention, the idea of the Gorsedd — an association of poets, writers, musicians and artists — soon caught on. The first gathering was held, of all places, at London's Primrose Hill in 1792. By 1819, Iolo had persuaded a Welsh eisteddfod at Carmarthen to adopt the idea.

The Gorsedd has subsequently become an important national institution within Wales. Its rituals and ceremonies, attended by gold, white, blue and green robed druids, reach a peak of symbolic importance during the Chairing of the Bard, the winning poet at the Royal National Eisteddfod. This annual event, held alternately in North and South Wales each August, is Wales's most important festival of traditional culture. The ceremonial side of the proceedings is only one element in a week of competitions which play a valuable — some say crucial — role in the preservation and fostering of the Welsh language (a tongue now spoken by only one-fifth of Wales's two-and-three-quarter-million inhabitants).

However historically spurious the ceremonial side may be, the eisteddfod's cultural importance is enormous, for the Royal National stands at the peak of a pyramid of events large and small, regional and local, formal and informal held throughout Wales. The movement has also spilled over into other, non-traditional areas, most notably at the Llangollen International Eisteddfod which attracts participants from all over the world.

PISTYLL RHAEADR WATERFALL
Clwyd

The narrow road which ventures north-west into the Berwyn Mountains from Llanrhaeadr-ym-Mochnant travels as far as Pistyll Rhaeadr and no further. The tarmac ends where the valley pinches itself into a block end of near-vertical slopes, a scene pervaded by the sound of water crashing onto rocks.

Pistyll Rhaeadr plunges for 240 ft over its mountain ledge into a gloomy, rocky and tree-shrouded dingle. One of the so-called 'Seven Wonders of Wales', it is the highest Welsh waterfall (and amongst the highest in Britain). The indefatigable George Borrow, 19th-century author of *Wild Wales*, naturally found his way to Pistyll Rhaeadr, recounting 'I never saw water falling so gracefully, so much like thin beautiful threads as here.'

Llanrhaeadr-ym-Mochnant is a peaceful country village on the doorstep of the empty Berwyns, bare-flanked mountains which rise to a summit of 2713 ft at Moel Sych, just over one mile north of Pistyll Rhaeadr. Whilst serving as rector in Llanrhaeadr from 1578 to 1588, William Morgan, later Bishop Morgan, worked on his historic first translation of the whole of the Bible into Welsh.

🚗 *PISTYLL RHAEADR is 4 miles north-west of Llanrhaeadr-ym-Mochnant, a village on the B4580 approximately 12 miles west of Oswestry.*

RHUDDLAN
Clwyd

Two very different historic sites capture the attention here. Rhuddlan Castle stands on a rise above the River Clwyd. Its powerful round towers, part of a clever ring of concentric defences, played their part in the English conquest of North Wales, for Rhuddlan was one of the chain of mighty castles built by Edward I in the late 13th century.

Of particular interest here was the monumental effort required to give the castle access to the sea, an important strategic advantage in Edward's days. The artificial-looking course of the Clwyd here betrays the fact that it first had to be made navigable by digging a deep-water passage over two miles long to the sea.

Bodrhyddan Hall, a mile or so east of the town, belongs to another era. The oldest part of this fine old red-bricked manor house dates from the late 17th century. Inside, Bodrhyddan is noteworthy for its extensive collection of weaponry and armour, two suits of which are believed to date from the Wars of the Roses.

🚗 *RHUDDLAN is at the junction of the A525, A547, and A5151, 2 miles south-east of Rhyl.*

RHYL AND PRESTATYN
Clwyd

There is not a lot that can be said about this pair of straightforward seaside resorts. No such reticence seems to have afflicted our verbose Victorian forbears, besotted as they were by the exaggerations and superlatives of purple prose. This is what an early tourist guidebook had to say about Rhyl: 'Its record of sunshine is known all over the world to be unique. While the big towns and cities are reeking with fog, Rhyl is bathed in warm sunshine, and it is no uncommon thing to see people bathing in the open sea as late as the middle of November.'

This resort still advertises itself as 'Sunny Rhyl', though it no longer

The Clwyd, canalised here to give Rhuddlan Castle sea-borne access

relies on the fickle British climate nor the ambitious claims of copywriters. Rhyl's purpose-built Sun Centre, a multi-leisure complex on the promenade, has its own mini-climate which makes November bathing here a less than chilly prospect.

'The old stigma of lack of amusements has now been entirely removed,' continued the old guidebook. For once, this is something of an understatement, for amusements have taken over well and truly in this unpretentious and uncomplicated resort, cast in the traditional British mould.

It is more of the same a few miles to the east of Prestatyn. A string of caravan parks and one or two holiday camps — re-christened holiday centres by the image-conscious tourism marketeers of the Eighties — spread themselves out behind the promenade and long sandy beach. With such a preponderance of insubstantial, impermanent development, it is somehow inappropriate that Prestatyn marks the northern end of Offa's Dyke, the great 8th-century earthwork that ran the length of Wales and still survives almost to its original height in parts (see special feature, page 71).

RHYL AND PRESTATYN are both on the A548 coast road between Colwyn Bay and Queensferry.

RUTHIN
Clwyd

The Council for British Archaeology considers Ruthin 'unique in North Wales for its number of timber-framed buildings'. This small market town, one of the prettiest in Wales, provides an architectural feast for those whose appetites incline to the 'magpie' half-timbered style of building.

Clustered around St Peter's Square in the middle of town is a striking array of black-and-white facades, enlivened by a jumble of gables and red-tiled roofs with a profusion of dormer windows. The banks even enter into the spirit of things. Both the National Westminster and Barclays do business behind timbered frontages, the former occupying Ruthin's old court house and prison. *Maen Huail* ('Huail's Stone'), beside Barclays, has gory Arthurian connections: on this large limestone block, King Arthur is said to have had Huail, his rival in love, beheaded.

The 180-ft spire of St Peter's Church dominates the square. Dating from the 14th century, it boasts a magnificent oak roof decorated with fine carving.

Ruthin, standing at the head of the fertile Vale of Clwyd, has been a prosperous market town for many centuries. The first Tuesday in each month sees a bustling street market, whilst livestock sales are held here twice weekly each Thursday and Friday.

The town's historic ambience has been a springboard for 'medieval Wednesdays', held throughout the summer months, during which period costume is much in evidence and appropriate entertainments are staged. The historic veracity of the so-called 'medieval' banquets, held nightly at the Ruthin Castle Hotel, can also be called into question; though it is perhaps churlish to do so, for these raucous events give pleasure to many. One medieval custom which does survive, authentic to this day, is the ringing at eight o'clock each evening of the Curfew Bell tolls, a practice continuously adhered to since the 11th century.

Little is left of Ruthin's medieval castle. Fragments of original stonework are incorporated into the masonry of a largely Victorian mansion which now serves as the aforementioned hotel.

RUTHIN is at the junction of the A525 and A494, about 17 miles north-west of Wrexham.

ST ASAPH
Clwyd

St Asaph vies with St David's for the title of 'smallest city'. Smallness seems to characterise this city-village. Its cathedral, probably the smallest in Britain, was established in 560 by St Kentigern, St Asaph taking over when the founding missionary returned to his native Scotland.

The cathedral suffers from faint praise. 'Though not large, (it) has something of dignity and grandeur', were Dr Johnson's qualified comments in 1774. Its exterior, admittedly plain and modest, belies the feeling of spaciousness inside and the extensive views that can be enjoyed from the tower (unusually for Welsh cathedrals, this one stands high on a hill).

Outside is an elaborate monument to the important 16th-century religious figure Bishop William Morgan, translator of the Bible into Welsh. He is buried within the cathedral, which also contains a museum displaying an unusual miscellany of artefacts.

ST ASAPH is on the A525, 6 miles south of Rhyl.

WREXHAM
Clwyd

The centre of this large town cannot claim to be well endowed with visitor attractions; apart, that is, from the magnificent early 16th-century tower which adorns the Church of St Giles. This tower is one of the much-quoted 'Seven Wonders of Wales':

'Pistyll Rhaeadr and Wrexham Steeple,
Snowdon's mountain, without its people;
Overton Yewtrees, Saint Winifred Wells,
Llangollen Bridge and Gresford Bells.'

Confidence in this highly contentious list is not inspired by the fact

St Asaph Cathedral, more impressive inside than out

that the 'wonders' are all confined to North Wales. However, this should not detract from the splendour of the tower, and the church which it graces.

The graveyard contains the tomb of Elihu Yale (d.1721) who lived near Wrexham in his later life. Yale is familiar, of course, thanks to the American university named after this generous benefactor (the campus even contains a reproduction of Wrexham tower). Part of the long epitaph on his grave reads:

'Born in America, in Europe bred,
In Africa travell'd, and in Asia wed,
Where long he liv'd and thriv'd;
at London dead.'

Wrexham contains isolated examples of architecture which reflect its former grandeur as a flourishing market, industrial and social centre. Its great treasure, though, lies on the outskirts of town. Erddig is a country house with a difference. Although it has its finery, this late 17th-century house, set in 938 acres, is mainly important for the authentic insight it gives into 'upstairs, downstairs' life on a country estate.

The master-servant relationship is brought to life in a house where the kitchen and working outbuildings are as well preserved — and as full of interest — as, for example, the period furniture in gilt and silver and superb state bed in Chinese silk. We also learn that the relationship at Erddig was, perhaps untypically, not an unhappy one. The Yorkes, owners of Erddig from 1773 to 1973 (when it was handed over to the National Trust), held their staff in high regard, even commissioning paintings of generations of servants which still hang on the walls today.

WREXHAM, near the Wales/England border, is 12 miles south-west of Chester.

The butler's pantry, Erddig, the definitive 'upstairs, downstairs' house

Index

INDEX

Acknowledgements
AA Picture Library: title verso, 6, 11, 32, 42/3, 79, 81, 82
Janet and Colin Bord: contents, 13(r), 14, 22/3, 25, 100, 101
Wales Tourist Board: endpapers, title page, 2, 4, 5, 8, 10, 12, 13 (l), 16/7, 18/9, 20(l,r), 21, 24, 26/7, 28/9, 29, 30, 31 (l,r), 33, 34, 36, 38, 39, 40, 41, 44, 45, 46/7, 47, 48, 49, 50 (l,r), 51 (l,r), 52, 54, 55, 56, 57, 58(l,r), 60, 61, 62, 63, 64, 66/7, 68, 69, 70, 71, 72, 74, 75, 76, 77, 80, 83, 84, 86, 87, 88, 90, 91, 92/3, 94, 95, 96, 97, 98, 99, 102, 104, 105, 106, 107, 108, 109(l,r), 110, 111, 112, 113

DISCARDED.